Workbook

Maths 2B
3rd Edition

Dr Fong Ho Kheong • Chelvi Ramakrishnan • Michelle Choo

Preface

My Pals Are Here! Maths (3rd Edition) is a comprehensive, task-based and learner-centred programme designed to provide pupils with a solid foundation in mathematics and opportunities to become efficient problem solvers.

For the Teacher:

Use **Practice** exercises with graded questions to test and reinforce concepts learnt in the Pupil's Book. Questions marked with an asterisk (*) are intermediate questions meant to stimulate pupils' thinking.

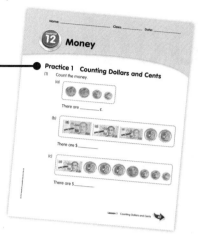

NEW! At the end of each chapter, assess pupils' knowledge and conceptual understanding using **Performance Tasks** that involve the use of manipulatives and other concrete materials.

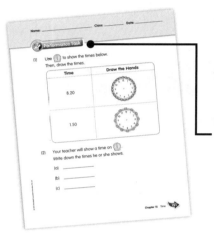

Develop pupils' creative and critical thinking skills with higher-order and non-routine questions in **Put on Your Thinking Cap!**

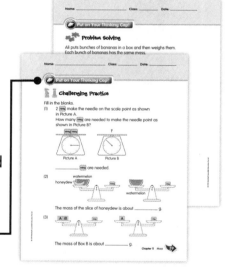

Reviews after every few chapters provide consolidation of concepts learnt.

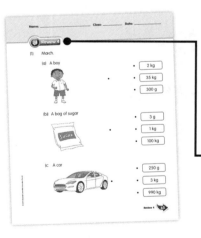

For the Pupil:

Share your thoughts with your teachers, create your own mathematics questions and become aware of your own mathematical thinking in **Maths Journal**!

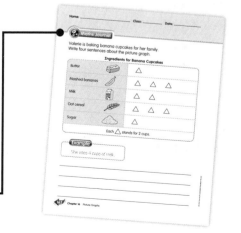

Enjoy learning mathematics with **My Pals Are Here! Maths (3rd Edition)**!

CONTENTS

10 Two-Step Word Problems: Addition and Subtraction
Practice 1 Two-Step Word Problems — 1
Maths Journal — 7
Performance Task — 8
Put on Your Thinking Cap! — 9

11 Mass
Practice 1 Getting to Know Masses — 11
Practice 2 Measuring in Kilograms — 13
Practice 3 Measuring in Grams — 19
Practice 4 Addition and Subtraction of Masses — 29
Practice 5 Multiplication and Division of Masses — 33
Maths Journal — 37
Performance Task — 38
Put on Your Thinking Cap! — 39

12 Money
Practice 1 Counting Dollars and Cents — 41
Practice 2 Changing Cents and Dollars — 49
Practice 3 Comparing Amounts of Money — 51
Practice 4 Word Problems — 55
Maths Journal — 60
Performance Task — 61
Put on Your Thinking Cap! — 63

Review 4 — 65

13 Two-Dimensional and Three-Dimensional Figures
Practice 1 Shapes and Two-Dimensional Figures — 73
Practice 2 Solids and Three-Dimensional Figures — 87
Practice 3 Making Patterns — 91
Maths Journal — 95
Performance Task — 96
Put on Your Thinking Cap! — 97

14 Fractions
Practice 1 Understanding Fractions — 99
Practice 2 More Fractions — 107
Practice 3 Comparing and Ordering Fractions — 109
Practice 4 Addition and Subtraction of Like Fractions — 117
Maths Journal — 125
Performance Task — 126
Put on Your Thinking Cap! — 127

Review 5 — 129

15 Time
Practice 1 Reading and Writing Time — 137
Practice 2 Learning a.m. and p.m. — 141
Practice 3 Time Taken in Hours and Minutes — 145
Maths Journal — 150
Performance Task — 151
Put on Your Thinking Cap! — 153

16 Picture Graphs
Practice 1 Reading Picture Graphs with Scales — 155
Maths Journal — 162
Performance Task — 163
Put on Your Thinking Cap! — 164

17 Volume
Practice 1 Getting to Know Volume — 167
Practice 2 Measuring in Litres — 171
Practice 3 Addition and Subtraction of Volumes — 175
Practice 4 Multiplication and Division of Volumes — 179
Maths Journal — 181
Performance Task — 182
Put on Your Thinking Cap! — 183

Revision 2 — 185

Two-Step Word Problems: Addition and Subtraction

Practice 1 Two-Step Word Problems

Solve.

(1) Uncle Sayid had 78 boxes of oranges and 130 boxes of peaches. After selling some boxes of peaches, he had 159 boxes of fruits left.

(a) How many boxes of fruits did Uncle Sayid have at first?

(b) How many boxes of peaches did Uncle Sayid sell?

(a)

![bar model with oranges and peaches sections, empty boxes above each, ? below total]

Uncle Sayid had _____ boxes of fruits at first.

(b)

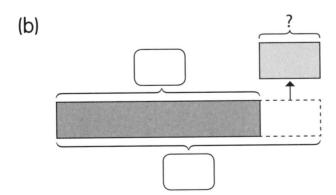

Uncle Sayid sold _____ boxes of peaches.

Lesson 1 Two-Step Word Problems

(2) Raihana has 356 movie tickets in her collection. Lila has 192 more movie tickets than Raihana. How many movie tickets do they have altogether?

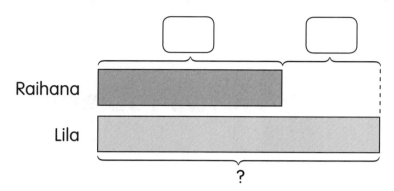

Lila has _____ movie tickets.

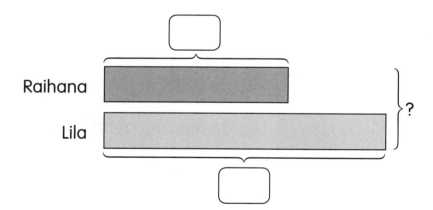

They have _____ movie tickets altogether.

Solve.

(3) There are 784 pupils in Excel Primary School.
325 pupils are boys.

(a) How many girls are there in the school?
(b) How many more girls than boys are there?

(a)

(b)

Lesson 1   Two-Step Word Problems

(4) Mrs Lim had $245.
She spent $78 and gave $36 to her son.
How much money did Mrs Lim have in the end?

First, find how much Mrs Lim had left after spending $78.

* (5) A cupboard is 197 cm tall.
It is 109 cm taller than a shelf.
What is the total height of the cupboard and the shelf?

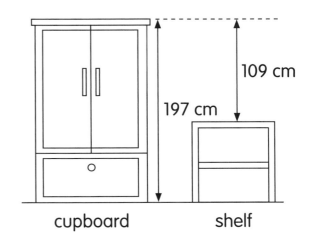

* (6)   Bernard ran 276 m.
He ran 148 m less than Melissa.
Melissa ran 116 m more than Joshua.
How far did Joshua run?

Name: _____ Class: _____ Date: _____

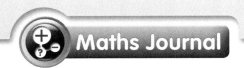 **Maths Journal**

Complete the word problem for the models below.
You may use the words in the box.
Show how you solve the word problem.

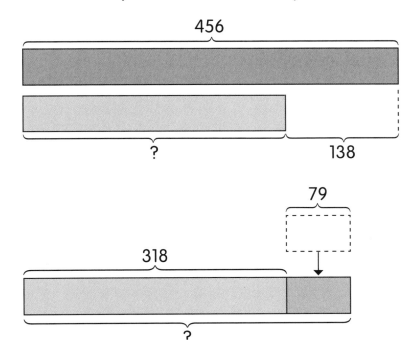

| buys another 79 buttons | Bruce | buttons |
| Nancy | how many buttons | have now |

Nancy has 456 buttons.

Bruce has 138 fewer buttons than Nancy.

_____

_____

_____

Chapter 10 Two-Step Word Problems: Addition and Subtraction

Name: _____ Class: _____ Date: _____

Write a word problem using the words in the box.
Use to show the model.
Then, solve.

| 6 charity tickets | they | Yuna sells | charity tickets |
| how many | altogether | Alex | 5 more charity tickets |

_____

_____

_____

They sell _____ charity tickets altogether.

Chapter 10 Two-Step Word Problems: Addition and Subtraction

Put on Your Thinking Cap!

 Challenging Practice

Gordon has some mangoes.
He throws 15 rotten mangoes away.
He buys another 37 mangoes.
He now has 96 mangoes.
How many mangoes does Gordon have at first?

Gordon has _____ mangoes at first.

Name: _____ Class: _____ Date: _____

 Problem Solving

Sally has 475 beads.
She has 250 more beads than Rachel.
Ain has 225 more beads than Rachel.
How many beads does Ain have?

Ain has _____ beads.

Chapter 10 Two-Step Word Problems: Addition and Subtraction

Chapter 11 Mass

Practice 1 Getting to Know Masses

(1) Fill in the blanks.

(a)

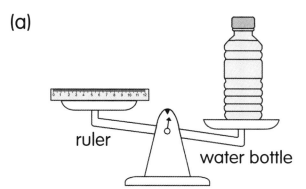

The _____ is heavier.

The _____ is lighter.

(b)

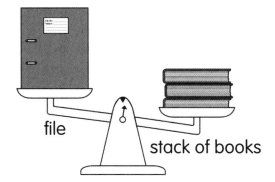

The _____ is heavier.

The _____ is lighter.

(2) Fill in the blanks.

(a) _____ is the heaviest.

(b) _____ is the lightest.

(3) Fill in the blanks.

(a) The _____ is the lightest.

(b) The _____ is the heaviest.

Chapter 11 Mass

Practice 2 Measuring in Kilograms

(1) Fill in the blanks.
Use the words in the box.

| more than | less than | as heavy as |
| tub of yogurt | cake | pear |

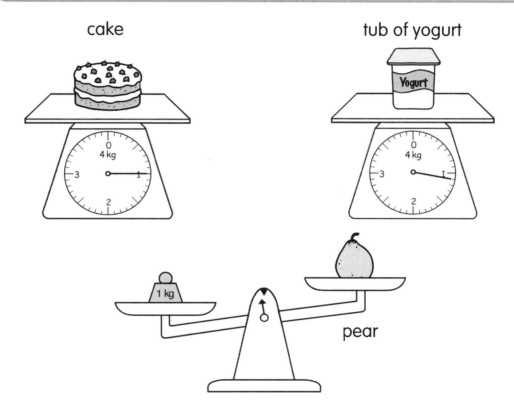

(a) The cake is _____ 1 kg.

(b) The mass of the pear is _____ 1 kg.

(c) The mass of the tub of yogurt is _____ 1 kg.

(d) The _____ is the lightest.

(e) The _____ is the heaviest.

Lesson 2 Measuring in Kilograms **13**

(2) Read each scale.
Then, write the mass.

(a) bag of sugar

_____ kg

(b) bag of rice

_____ kg

(c) watermelon

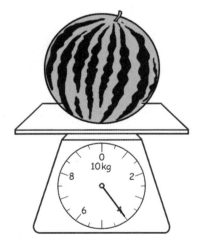

_____ kg

(d) bag of potatoes

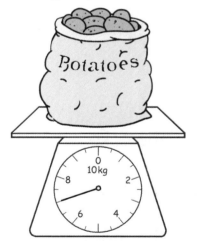

_____ kg

(3) Fill in the blanks.

bag of oranges   bag of potatoes

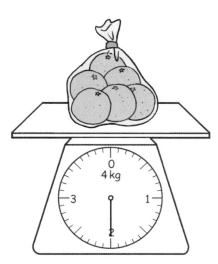 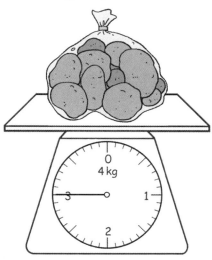

(a) The mass of the bag of oranges is _____ kg.

(b) The mass of the bag of potatoes is _____ kg.

(c) Which bag is heavier?

The bag of _____ is heavier.

(d) The bag of _____ is lighter than the bag

of _____ .

(4) Fill in the blanks.

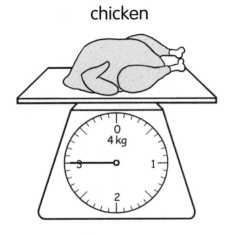
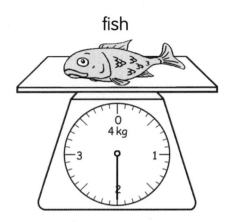
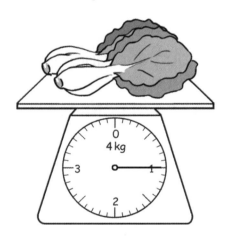

(a) The chicken weighs _____ kg.

(b) The vegetables weigh _____ kg.

(c) The fish weighs _____ kg.

(d) Which is heavier, the chicken or the vegetables?

The _____ is heavier.

Chapter 11 Mass

(e) Which is heavier, the chicken or the fish?

The _____ is heavier.

(f) Which is the heaviest?

The _____ is the heaviest.

(g) Which is the lightest?

The _____ are the lightest.

(h) Arrange the items from lightest to heaviest.

_____, _____, _____
lightest

(i)

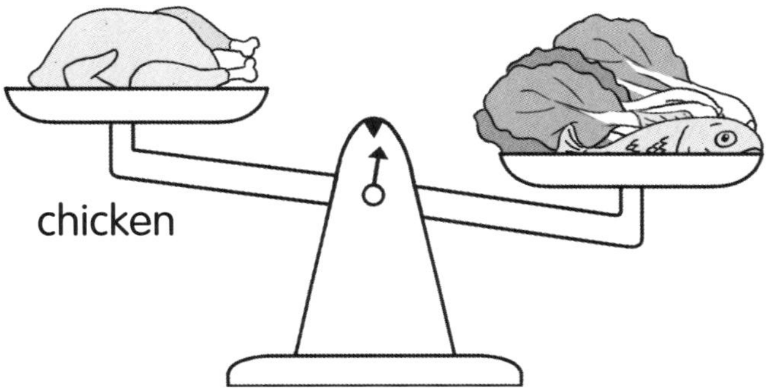

The items are put on a balance scale.

Do you think the picture above is correct? _____

Why?

_____

_____

Lesson 2 Measuring in Kilograms

*(5) Fill in the blanks.
The pictures show Ailing's mass and Roger's mass after lunch.

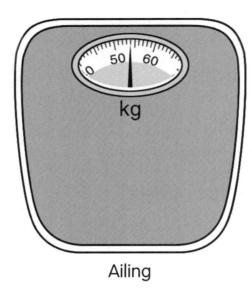
Ailing

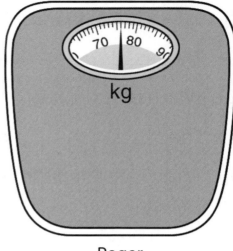
Roger

(a) The mass of Ailing is _____ kg.

(b) The mass of Roger is _____ kg.

(c) Who is heavier, Roger or Ailing?

_____ is heavier.

How much heavier? _____ kg

Practice 3 Measuring in Grams

(1) Fill in the blanks.
The mass of each 1g is 1 gram.

(a)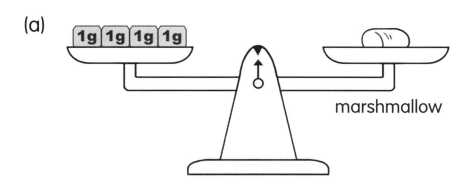

The mass of the piece of marshmallow is about

_____ g.

(b)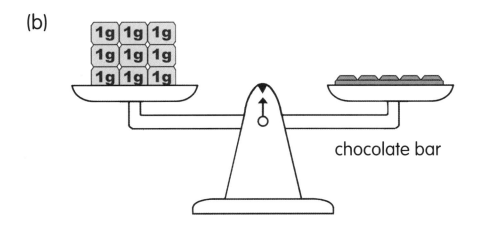

The mass of the chocolate bar is about _____ g.

(c)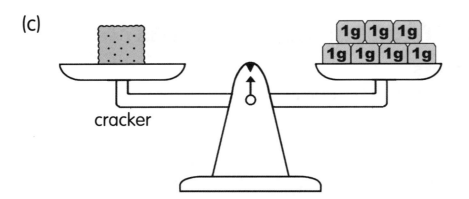

The mass of the cracker is about _____ g.

(d)

The mass of the cookie is about _____ g.

(2) Fill in the missing numbers.

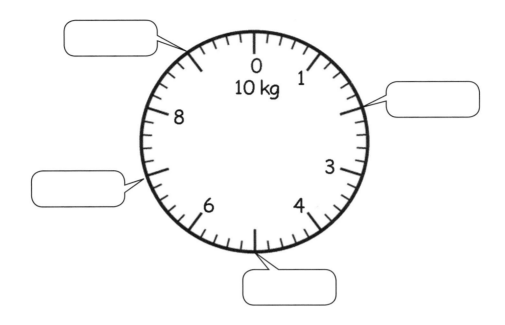

(3) Fill in the missing numbers.

(a)

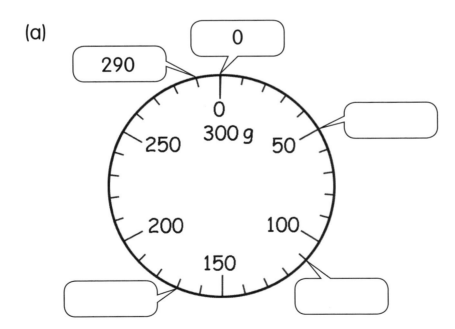

Lesson 3 Measuring in Grams

(b)

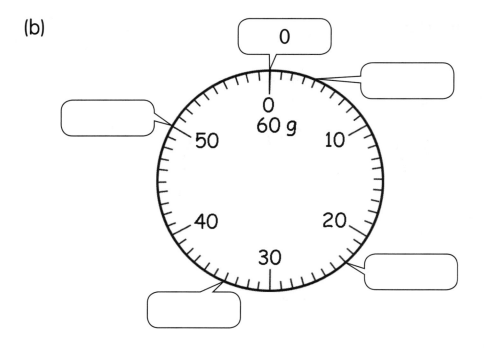

(c)

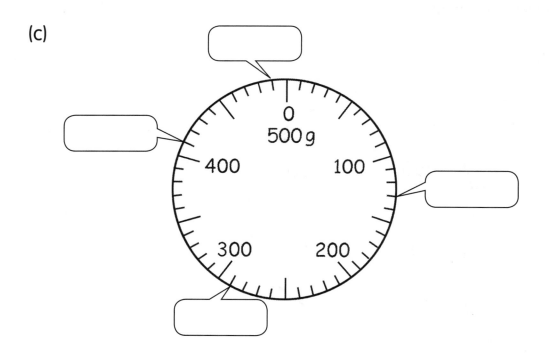

(4) Fill in the blanks.

(a)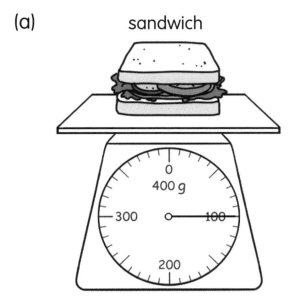

The mass of the sandwich is _____ g.

(b)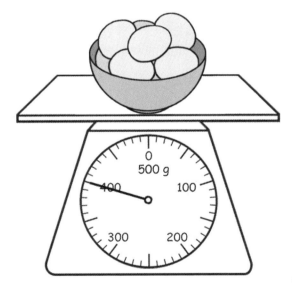

The mass of the bowl of eggs is _____ g.

Lesson 3   Measuring in Grams

(c) muffins

The mass of the muffins is _____ g.

(d) packet of biscuits

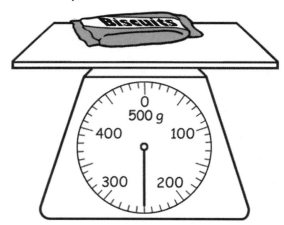

The mass of the packet of biscuits is _____ g.

(e) bag of peanuts

The mass of the bag of peanuts is _____ g.

(f) box of crackers

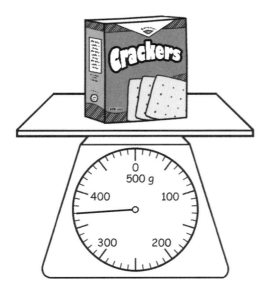

The mass of the box of crackers is _____ g.

(5) Fill in the blanks.

tray of eggs

bag of chips

box of biscuits

can of beans

(a) The mass of the tray of eggs is _____ g.

(b) The mass of the box of biscuits is _____ g.

(c) The _____ is the lightest.

(d) The _____ is the heaviest.

(e) Arrange the items from lightest to heaviest.

_____, _____, _____, _____
lightest

(6) Find the mass of each vegetable.
Fill in the blanks.

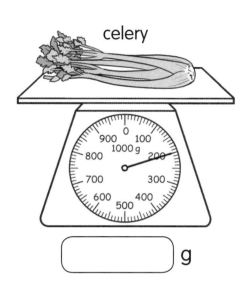

celery

_____ g

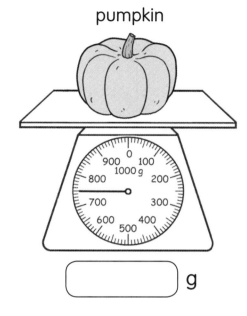

pumpkin

_____ g

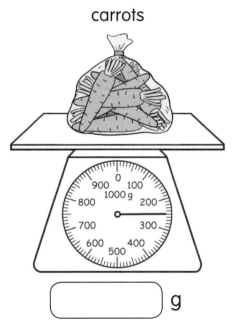

carrots

_____ g

peppers

_____ g

(a) The _____ is the heaviest.

(b) The _____ are the lightest.

*(c) The _____ is heavier than the bag of peppers.
It is also lighter than the bag of carrots.

Lesson 3 Measuring in Grams

(7) Look at the boxes.
Then, fill in the blanks.

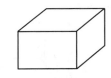

Box A
180 g

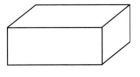

Box B
250 g

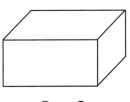

Box C
800 g

Box D
430 g

(a) Which is the heaviest? Box _____

(b) Which is the lightest? Box _____

Write **heavier** or **lighter** in the blanks.

(c) Box B is _____ than Box D.

(d) Box D is _____ than Box A.

Fill in the blanks.

(e) Arrange the boxes from lightest to heaviest.

_____, _____, _____, _____
lightest

Chapter 11 Mass

Name: _____ Class: _____ Date: _____

Practice 4 Addition and Subtraction of Masses

You may use models to help you solve the problems.

(1) Durian Seller A has 35 kg of durians.
Durian Seller B has 67 kg of durians.
What is the total mass of the durians?

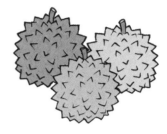

The total mass of the durians is _____ kg.

(2) Farmi weighs 32 kg.
He is 5 kg lighter than Sally.
What is Sally's mass?

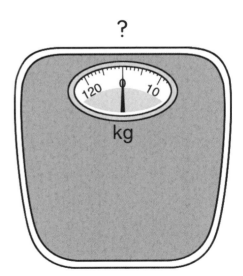

Sally's mass is _____ kg.

Lesson 4 Addition and Subtraction of Masses

(3) Mr Tan needs 400 g of flour to make a small cake.
He has only 143 g of flour.
How much more flour does he need?

He needs _____ g more flour.

(4) A restaurant had 90 kg of beef.
On Sunday, 56 kg of beef was sold.
How much beef was left in the restaurant on Monday?

_____ kg of beef was left in the restaurant on Monday.

(5) Ali weighs 25 kg.
Jinrong is 6 kg heavier than Ali.
What is their total mass?

Their total mass is _____ kg.

(6) Lizhen bought a bag of onions with a mass of 750 g.
She used 100 g of the onions for lunch.
She used 480 g of the onions for dinner.
How many grams of onions were left?

There were _____ g of onions left.

Lesson 4 Addition and Subtraction of Masses

(7) Mani sells 45 kg of rice on Monday.
He sells 18 kg less rice on Monday than on Tuesday.
How much rice does he sell altogether on the two days?

He sells _____ kg of rice altogether on the two days.

(8) A baker has 975 g of sugar.
He uses 250 g of sugar to bake some cookies and
another 600 g of sugar for some cakes.
How much sugar does he have left?

He has _____ g of sugar left.

Practice 5 Multiplication and Division of Masses

(1) The total mass of 5 bags of corn is 30 kg.
Each bag has the same mass.
What is the mass of each bag of corn?

The mass of each bag of corn is _____ kg.

(2) There are 6 birthday cakes.
Each birthday cake weighs 3 kg.
What is the total mass of the 6 birthday cakes?

The total mass of the 6 birthday cakes is _____ kg.

(3) A grape weighs 10 g.
What is the total mass of 7 such grapes?

The total mass of 7 such grapes is _____ g.

(4) The mass of a bag of flour is 2 kg.
Mr Muthu buys 8 bags of flour.
What is the total mass of flour that Mr Muthu buys?

The total mass of flour that Mr Muthu buys is _____ kg.

(5) The total mass of 3 packets of salt is 6 kg.
Each packet has the same mass.
What is the mass of each packet of salt?

The mass of each packet of salt is _____ kg.

(6) The total mass of some cherries is 36 g.
Each cherry weighs 4 g.
How many cherries are there?

There are _____ cherries.

Lesson 5   Multiplication and Division of Masses

(7) Mr Tan prepares 4 turkeys for a party.
Each turkey weighs 8 kg.
What is the total mass of the 4 turkeys?

The total mass of the 4 turkeys is _____ kg.

(8) The total mass of some ducks is 27 kg.
Each duck weighs 3 kg.
How many ducks are there?

There are _____ ducks.

Name: _____ Class: _____ Date: _____

Look at the pictures.
(1)   Write sentences to compare the mass of the boxes.
      Use the words **lighter**, **heavier**, **lightest** and **heaviest**.

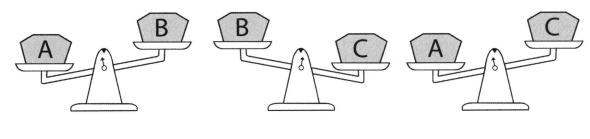

_____

_____

_____

_____

_____

_____

(2)   Arrange the boxes from heaviest to lightest.

      _____, _____, _____
        heaviest

Chapter 11   Mass

Name: _____ Class: _____ Date: _____

Performance Task

Use [1g], 3 small packets of beans and a balance scale.
Label the packets of beans A, B and C.
Weigh each packet of beans with [1g].
Then, fill in the blanks.

(a) The mass of A is about _____ g.

(b) The mass of B is about _____ g.

(c) The mass of C is about _____ g.

(d) The total mass of A and B is about _____ g.

(e) Compare any two packets of beans.

   _____ is heavier than _____.

   It is about _____ g heavier.

(f) Arrange the packets of beans from lightest to heaviest.

   _____, _____, _____
      lightest

(g) Write an addition or subtraction story about any two packets of beans.

   _____

   _____

   _____

Chapter 11 Mass

Name: _____ Class: _____ Date: _____

 Put on Your Thinking Cap!

 Challenging Practice

Fill in the blanks.

(1) 2 `100g` make the needle on the scale point as shown in Picture A.
How many `100g` are needed to make the needle point as shown in Picture B?

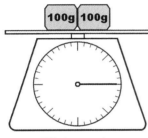 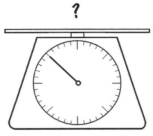

Picture A   Picture B

_____ `100g` are needed.

(2)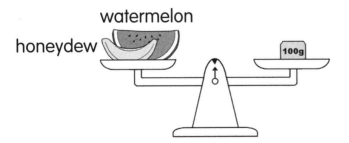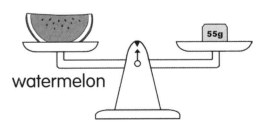

The mass of the slice of honeydew is about _____ g.

(3)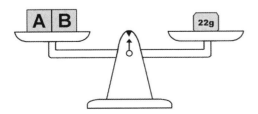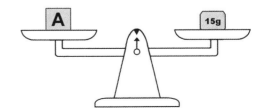

The mass of Box B is about _____ g.

Chapter 11 Mass

Name: _____ Class: _____ Date: _____

Put on Your Thinking Cap!

Problem Solving

Ali puts bunches of bananas in a box and then weighs them.
Each bunch of bananas has the same mass.

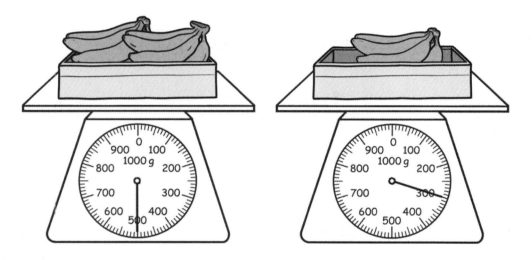

(a) What is the mass of the box and two bunches of bananas?

_____ g

(b) What is the mass of the box and one bunch of bananas?

_____ g

(c) What is the mass of one bunch of bananas?

(d) What is the mass of the box?

Chapter 12 Money

Practice 1 Counting Dollars and Cents

(1) Count the money.

(a)

There are _____ ¢.

(b)

There are $ _____.

(c)

There are $ _____.

(2) Fill in the blanks.

(a) $20.00 .... _____ dollars _____ cents

(b) $0.03 .... _____ dollars _____ cents

(c) $0.25 .... _____ dollars _____ cents

(d) $40.20 .... _____ dollars _____ cents

(e) $127.15 .... _____ dollars _____ cents

(3) Write the amount of money in two ways.

Example

__$10__ or __$10.00__

(a)

_____ or _____

(b)

_____ or _____

Chapter 12 Money

(4) Write the amount of money in two ways.

Example

65 ¢ or $ 0.65

(a)

_______¢ or $_______

(b)

$_______ or $_______

(c)

$_______ or $_______

(5) How much money is there?

Example

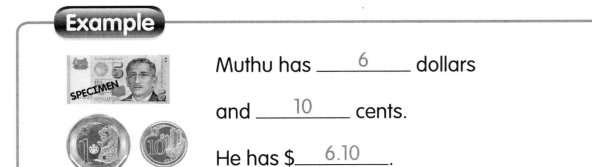

Muthu has ___6___ dollars and ___10___ cents.

He has $___6.10___.

(a)

Mrs Lim has _____ dollars and _____ cents.

She has $_____.

(b)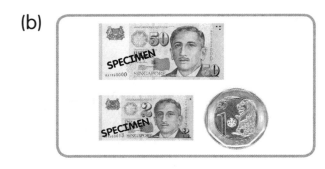

Sheila has _____ dollars and _____ cents.

She has $_____.

(c)

Paul has _____ dollars and _____ cents.

He has $_____.

Chapter 12   Money

(6) Match.

(a)  • $4.45

(b)  • $0.35

(c)  • $16.00

(d)  • $13.35

Lesson 1 Counting Dollars and Cents

(7) Whose money is this?
Circle the name of the correct owner.

(a)

Xiaojie has $2.06.

Muthu has $20.60.

Siti has $26.

(b)

John has $7.00.

Mary has $7.70.

Peter has $7.07.

(c)

Ali has $1.10.

Najib has $11.00.

Meiling has $0.11.

(d)

Nora has $0.65.

Susan has $5.15.

Osman has $50.15.

Chapter 12   Money

(8) Show the amount of money in two ways.

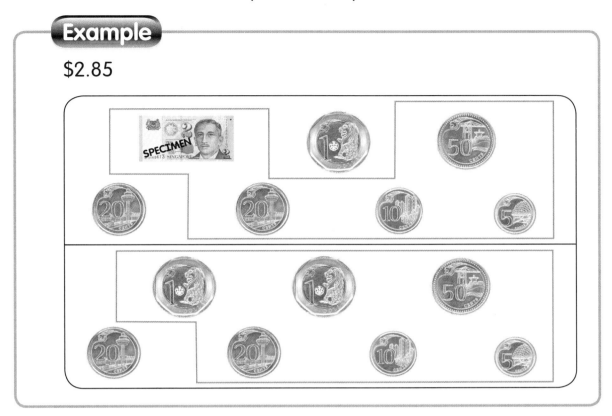

$2.85

(a) $3.60

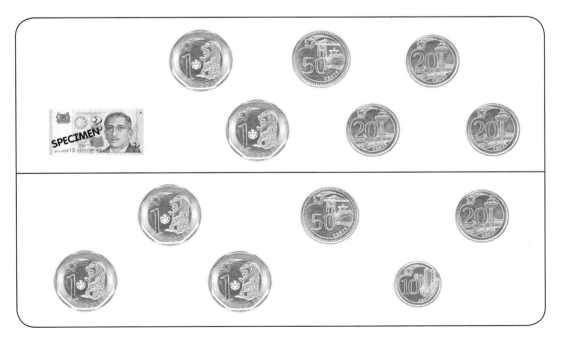

Lesson 1 Counting Dollars and Cents

(b) $75.20

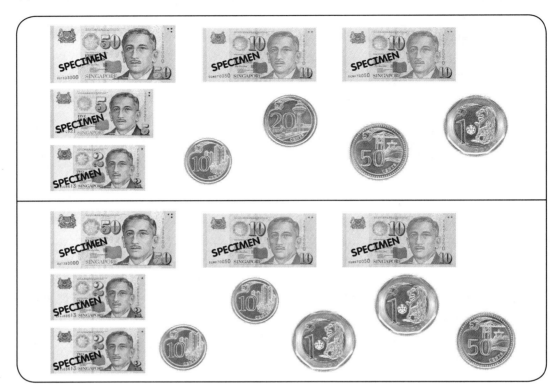

(c) $114.30

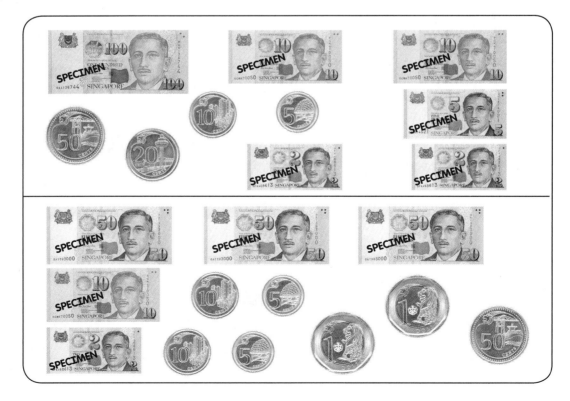

Chapter 12 Money

Practice 2   Changing Cents and Dollars

(1) Write the amount of money in two ways.

Example

$__2.20__ or __220__¢

(a)

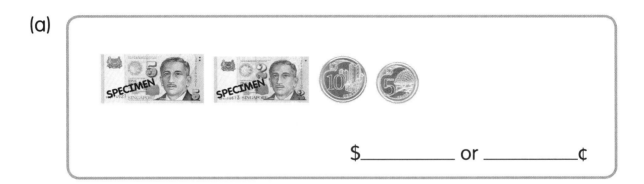

$_____ or _____¢

(b)

$_____ or _____¢

(c)

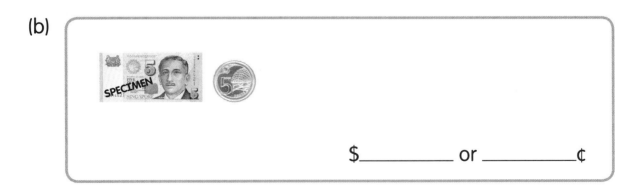

$_____ or _____¢

(2) Write the cents in dollars.

(a) 20¢ $ __0.20__   (b) 120¢ $ _____

(c) 543¢ $ _____   (d) 106¢ $ _____

(e) 350¢ $ _____   (f) 83¢ $ _____

(g) 17¢ $ _____   (h) 2¢ $ _____

(3) Write the dollars in cents.

(a) $4.80   __480__ ¢   (b) $3.51   _____ ¢

(c) $6.95   _____ ¢   (d) $1.05   _____ ¢

(e) $0.44   _____ ¢   (f) $0.69   _____ ¢

(g) $8   _____ ¢   (h) $10   _____ ¢

Name: _____   Class: _____   Date: _____

Practice 3   Comparing Amounts of Money

(1) Compare the amounts.
Complete the charts.
Then, fill in the blanks.

(a) A story book costs $14.20.
A toy car costs $15.00.

Dollars	Cents
14	20

Dollars	Cents
15	0

$_____ is more than $_____.

$_____ is less than $_____.

Which item costs more? _____

(b) Limei saved $70.80.

Dollars	Cents

Jeremy saved $70.95.

Dollars	Cents

$_____ is more than $_____.

$_____ is less than $_____.

Who saved more? _____

Lesson 3   Comparing Amounts of Money   51

(c) Chinwee has $45.70.

Dollars	Cents

Jackson has $45.15.

Dollars	Cents

Nat has $45.45.

Dollars	Cents

Do all of them have the same amount of money? _____

$_____ is the greatest amount.

$_____ is the smallest amount.

Who has the most amount of money? _____

Who has the least amount of money? _____

(d)

Shelf

Bicycle

Pair of shoes

Which item costs the most amount of money? _____

Which item costs the least amount of money? _____

(2) Write the amount of money in each set.
Then, tick (✓) the set that has a greater amount.

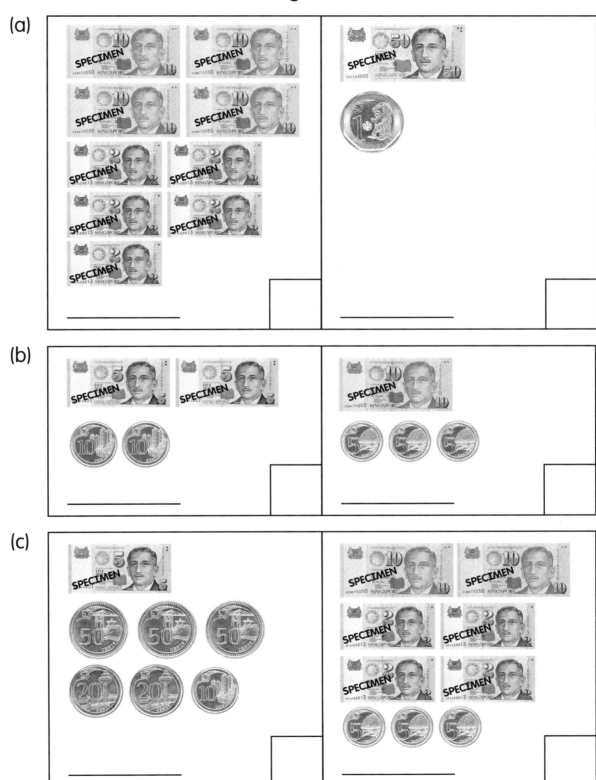

Lesson 3   Comparing Amounts of Money

(3) Circle the smaller amount.   (4) Circle the greater amount.

(a) $3.85 $4.10   (a) $28.90 $27.95

(b) $62.40 $62.25   (b) $71.09 $7.90

(5) Compare the amounts.

| $27.45 | $27.90 | $37.05 |
| Customer A | Customer B | Customer C |

(a) Which customer paid the most? _____

(b) Which customer paid the least? _____

(6) Look at the advertisement.
    Then, fill in the blanks.

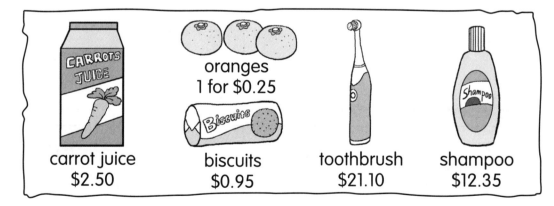

carrot juice $2.50   biscuits $0.95   toothbrush $21.10   shampoo $12.35
oranges 1 for $0.25

(a) Which item is the most expensive? _____

(b) Which item is the cheapest? _____

(c) Name an item that costs more than $10. _____

(d) Name an item that costs less than $1. _____

Chapter 12 Money

Practice 4 Word Problems

Use models to help you solve the problems.

(1) Anand bought a stick of fish balls for 75¢.
He gave the cashier $1.
How much change did he receive?

(2) Erfan has $20.
He buys a watermelon for $6.
How much money has he left?

(3) Cuifen had $730.
She gave $200 to her mother.
Then, her father gave her $250.
How much did Cuifen have in the end?

(4) Ben had $460 in his savings at first.
He saved $200 in January.
He saved another $150 in February.
How much savings did Ben have at the end of February?

(5) Mrs Khan bought a jacket for $50.
She bought a dress that cost $12 more.
How much did she pay altogether?

(6) Mrs Fan had $600. She had $187 more than Mrs Bala.
Mr Woods had $501.
How much more did Mr Woods have than Mrs Bala?

Lesson 4 Word Problems

(7) Mrs Rajan gives $2 to Muthu as his allowance every day.
What is Muthu's total allowance from Monday to Friday?

(8) Mr Lim gives $40 to his grandchildren.
Each of them receives $5.
How many grandchildren does he have?

(9) Mrs Tan bought 4 bottles of chilli sauce.
Each bottle cost $4.
How much did she pay altogether?

(10) Aminah had $50.
She spent all her money on 5 bags.
The cost of each bag was the same.
How much did each bag cost?

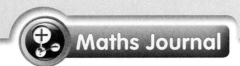 Maths Journal

Kassim made some mistakes in his homework.
Help him to correct the mistakes.

Example

Kassim's mistake: 35¢ = $3.50

Correct answer: 35¢ = $0.35 or
                 350¢ = $3.50

(a) Kassim's mistake: One dollar and sixty cents = $1.06

Correct answer: _____

(b) Kassim's mistake: 450¢ = $450

Correct answer: _____

(c) Kassim's mistake: $6 is $5 less than $1.

Correct answer: _____

(d) Kassim's mistake: $90 is $10 more than $100.

Correct answer: _____

Chapter 12 Money

Performance Task

(1) Use  to show these amounts.

(a) 45¢

(b) $3.70

(c) $25.30

Chapter 12 Money

(2) Mary had $55.
She wanted to buy a doll and a sharpener.

Mary saw two dolls and two sharpeners that she liked.

Doll A   Doll B   Sharpener A   Sharpener B

Use 🪙 to show the total cost of:

(a) Doll A and Sharpener A.

(b) Doll A and Sharpener B.

(c) Doll B and Sharpener A.

(d) Doll B and Sharpener B.

Mary spent **all** her money.

Which doll and sharpener did she buy?

_____

_____

_____

Chapter 12 Money

Name: _____ Class: _____ Date: _____

  Challenging Practice

Draw the amount of money using $5, $2, 20¢ and 10¢.
Show the least number of notes and coins needed to make the amount.

Example

$5.70

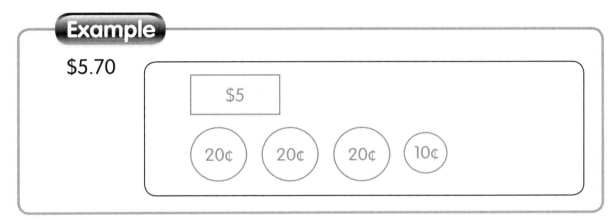

(1) $4.60

(2) $9.30

Chapter 12 Money 63

Name: _____ Class: _____ Date: _____

 Problem Solving

Draw three possible sets of notes and/or coins that Yasmin might have.
Use $10, $5, $2, $1, 50¢, 20¢ and 10¢.

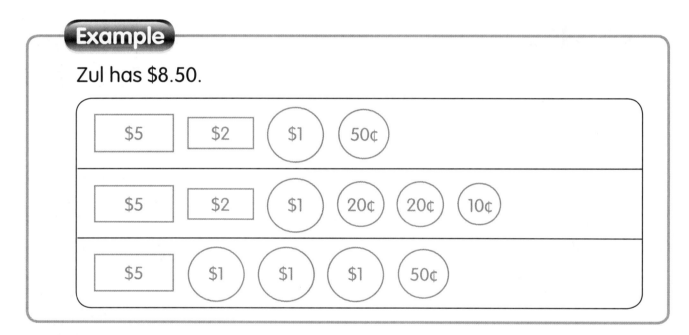

Yasmin has $27.50

Chapter 12 Money

Name: _____ Class: _____ Date: _____

(1) Match.

(a) A boy

- 2 kg
- 35 kg
- 300 g

(b) A bag of sugar

- 3 g
- 1 kg
- 100 kg

(c) A car

- 250 g
- 3 kg
- 990 kg

Review 4

(2) Fill in the blanks.

(a)

The vegetable weighs _____ g.

(b)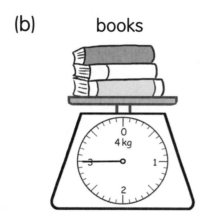

The books weigh _____ kg.

(3) Fill in the blank.

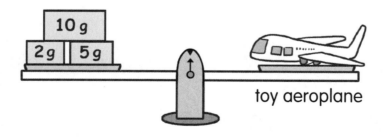

The mass of the toy aeroplane is about _____ g.

(4) Fill in the blanks.

(a) The chicken weighs _____ g.

(b) The duck weighs _____ g.

(c) Which is lighter?

The _____ is lighter.

(d) The _____ is heavier than the _____.

(5) Fill in the blank.

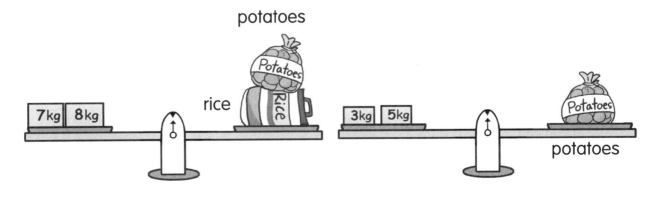

What is the mass of the bag of rice? About _____ kg

Review 4

(6) What is the mass of the cupcake?

The mass of the cupcake is _____ g.

(7) The mass of a bottle of oil is 2 kg.
What is the mass of 9 such bottles of oil?

The mass of 9 such bottles of oil is _____ kg.

(8) A bottle of milk weighs 450 g.
It is put into a box with a mass of 37 g.
What is the total mass of the bottle of milk and the box?

The total mass of the bottle of milk and the box is _____ g.

Solve. You may draw models to help you.

(9) Kimwee runs 400 m.
He runs 70 m less than Joey.
Sam runs 275 m.
How much farther does Joey run than Sam?

Joey runs _____ m farther than Sam.

(10) Junming's hand puppet weighs 440 g.
It is 120 g heavier than Hector's hand puppet.
What is the total mass of the two hand puppets?

The total mass of the two hand puppets is _____ g.

(11) Write the amount of money in dollars.

(a)

$ _____

(b)

$ _____

(c)

$ _____

(12) Write in dollars or cents.

(a) $7.00 = _____ ¢   (b) 910¢ = $_____

(c) $0.85 = _____ ¢   (d) 55¢ = $_____

(e) $0.06 = _____ ¢   (f) 10¢ = $_____

Review 4

(13) Billy has a $5 note.
He wants to buy a packet of juice that costs $1.
He also wants to buy a slice of honeydew that costs $2.
How much change will he receive?

He will receive $_____ change.

(14) Count the amount of money in each set.
Then, arrange the amounts of money from greatest to smallest.

(a)

$_____, $_____, $_____
greatest

(b)

$ _____

$ _____

$_____, $_____, $_____
greatest

Name: _____ Class: _____ Date: _____

Two-Dimensional and Three-Dimensional Figures

Practice 1 Shapes and Two-Dimensional Figures

(1) Colour the shapes.

> Circle — green   Triangle — yellow   Rectangle — purple
> Semicircle — blue   Quarter circle — red

Lesson 1 Shapes and Two-Dimensional Figures   73

(2) Cut out the grey circle at the bottom of this page.
Fold the circle into equal halves.
Cut it along the fold.
Paste the cut-outs in the box below.
You may also use the stickers at the back of the book.

These are called _____.

(3) Cut out the black circle at the bottom of this page.
Fold the circle into 4 equal parts.
Cut it along the folds.
Paste the cut-outs in the box below.
You may also use the stickers at the back of the book.

These are called _____.

Chapter 13   Two-Dimensional and Three-Dimensional Figures

(4) Trace the correct figures.

(a) Straight lines only

(b) Curves only

(c) Straight lines and curves

(5) Use the circles from the next page to make 2 semicircles and 4 quarter circles.
Make a picture using the cut-outs.
Paste them below.
You do not need to use all the pieces.
You may also use the stickers at the back of the book.

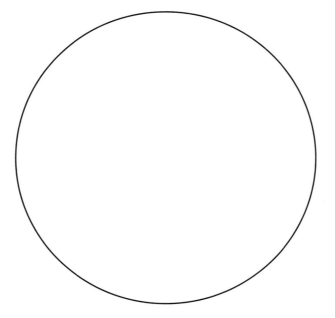
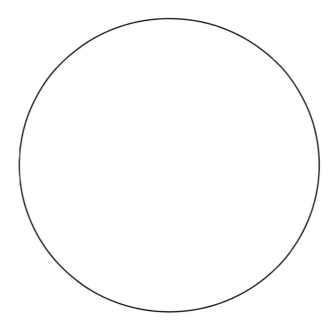

Lesson 1 Shapes and Two-Dimensional Figures 77

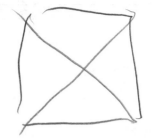

BLANK

(6) Cut out the shapes.
Paste them on top of the shapes given.
Here are two simple rules to follow:
(a) All cut-outs must be used.
(b) Cut-outs cannot overlap one another.
You may also use the stickers at the back of the book.

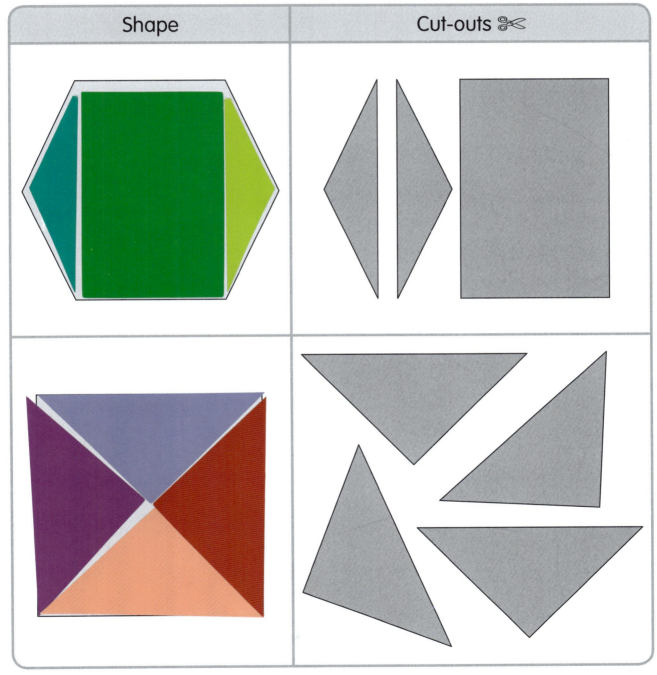

BLANK

(7) Cut out the shapes.
Paste them on top of the figures given.
Here are two simple rules to follow:
(a) All cut-outs must be used.
(b) Cut-outs cannot overlap one another.
You may also use the stickers at the back of the book.

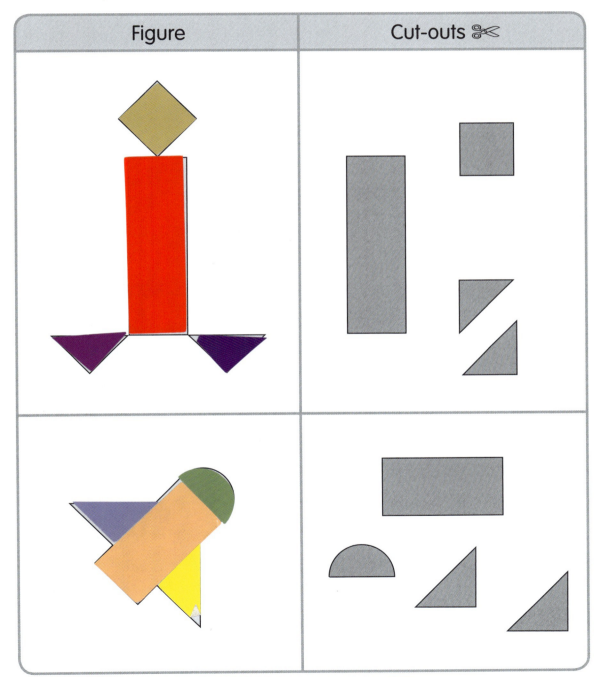

BLANK

(8) Each of the figures below is made up of two shapes.
Name the shapes.

(a) This figure is made up of

a __triangle__ and

a __rectangle__.

(b) This figure is made up of

a __samesercol__ and

a __corder__.

(9) Circle the correct figure.

(a) This figure is made up of a semicircle and a square.

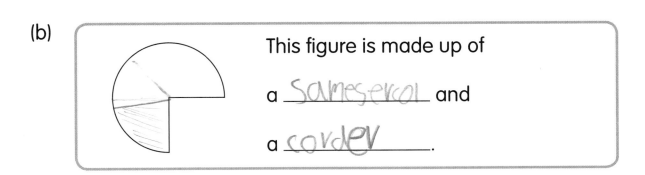

(b) This figure is made up of a rectangle and a circle.

Lesson 1 Shapes and Two-Dimensional Figures 83

(10) Copy these figures to the dot grids on the right.

Example

(a)

(b)

(c)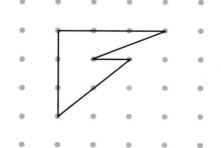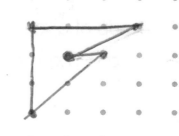

Chapter 13 Two-Dimensional and Three-Dimensional Figures

(11) Copy these figures to the square grids on the right.

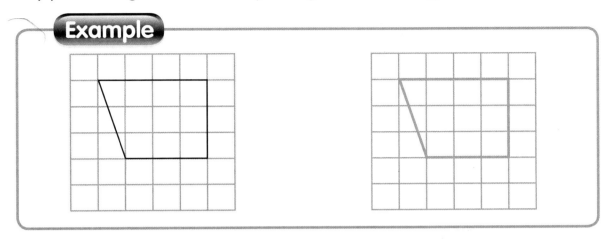

(a)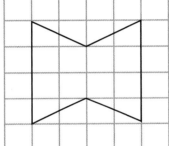

(b)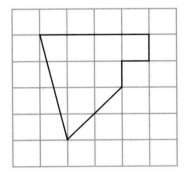

(c)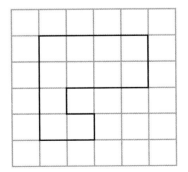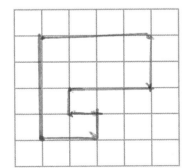

Lesson 1 Shapes and Two-Dimensional Figures

Name: _____ Class: _____ Date: _____

Maths Journal

(a) Draw a happy face using curves only.

(b) Draw a figure of a boy using straight lines and curves.

Chapter 13 Two-Dimensional and Three-Dimensional Figures

Practice 2 Solids and Three-Dimensional Figures

(1) Name these objects.
Use the words in the box.

| Cone | Cube | Cuboid |
| Cylinder | | Sphere |

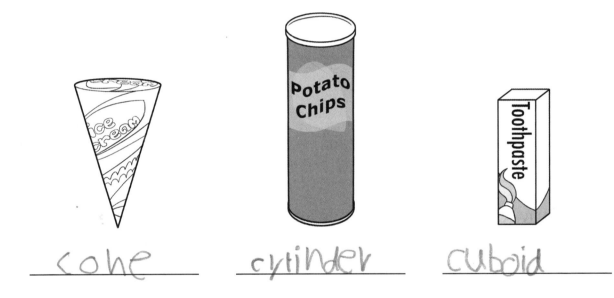

cone   cylinder   cuboid

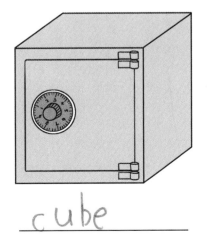
cube

sphere

Lesson 2 Solids and Three-Dimensional Figures

(2) Which of these objects have flat faces?
Which of these objects do not have flat faces?

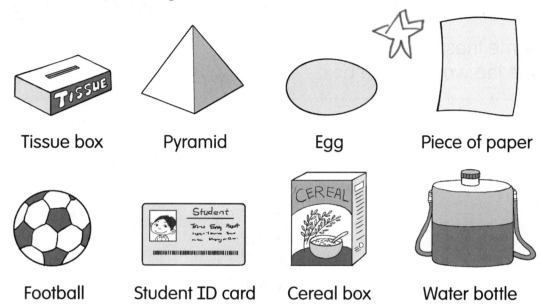

Write your answers below.

Have flat faces	Tissue box Pyramid Piece of Paper Student ID card cereal box Water bottle
Do not have flat faces	Football Egg

(3) Cut out 3 pictures of objects that have flat faces from newspapers or magazines.
Paste them in the space below.

Lesson 2 Solids and Three-Dimensional Figures

(4) Colour the solids used in each figure.

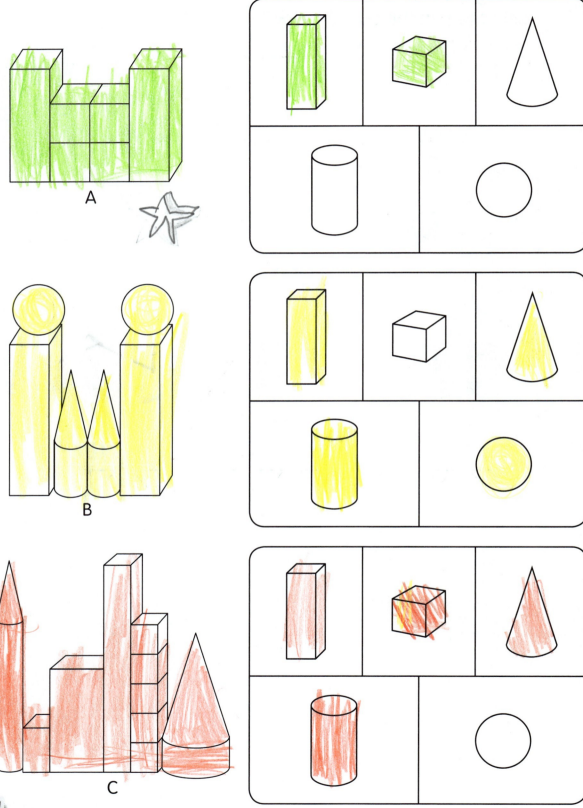

Practice 3 Making Patterns

(1) Circle the pattern that is repeated.

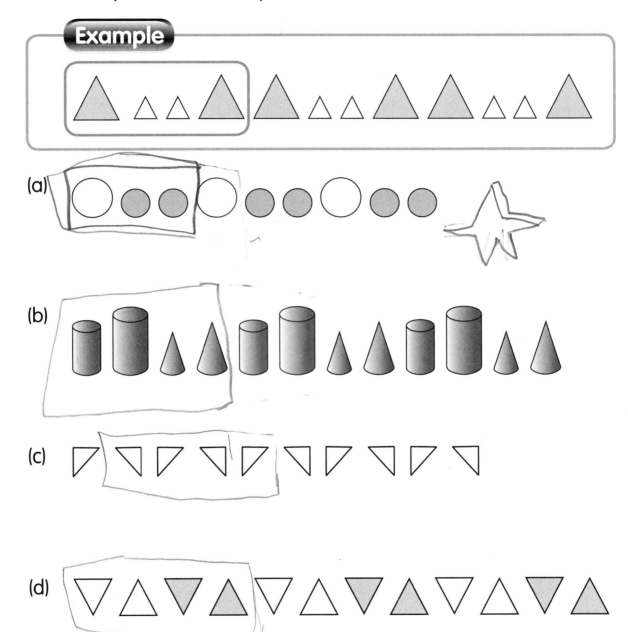

(2) Look at the pattern.
Circle what comes next.

Example

(a)

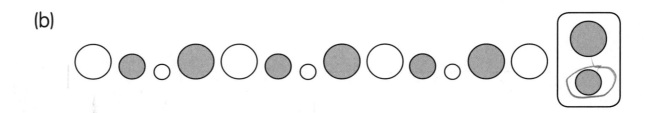

(b)

(c)

(3) Circle the correct figure to complete the pattern.

(a)

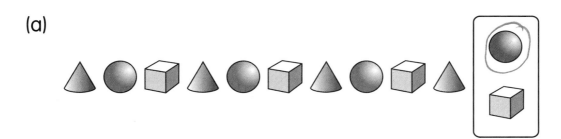

(b)

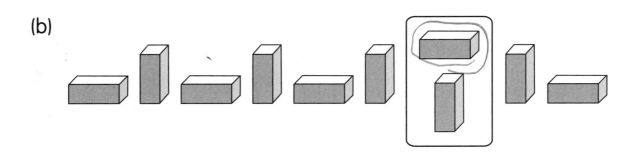

(c)

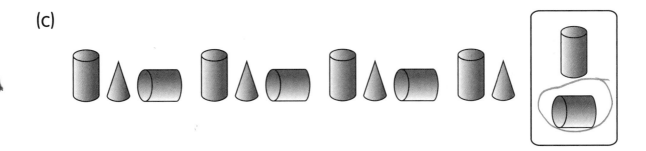

Lesson 3 Making Patterns 93

(d)

*(e)

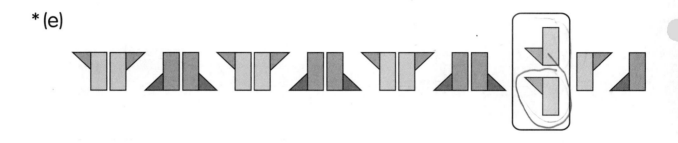

(f)

Chapter 13 Two-Dimensional and Three-Dimensional Figures

Name: _____ Class: _____ Date: _____

Maths Journal

(1) The pattern below is made with shapes.

    (a) Circle the mistake in the pattern.

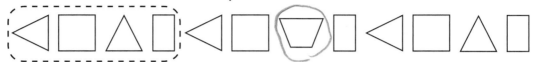

    (b) Which of the following is the correct shape?

    (c) Name the correct shape.

        Triangle

(2) The pattern below is made with solids.

    (a) Circle the mistake in the pattern.

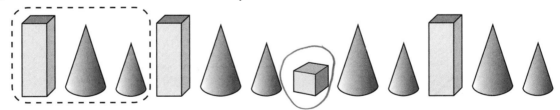

    (b) Which of the following is the correct solid?

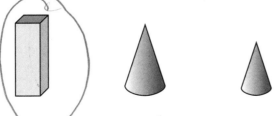

    (c) Name the correct solid.

        rectangular prisam

Chapter 13 Two-Dimensional and Three-Dimensional Figures

Performance Task

(1) Look at the two solids, X and Y, that are given to you.

    (a) Write the names of these solids.

        X: _____

        Y: _____

    (b) Look at the faces of Y.
        What is the shape(s) of the faces?

        _____

(2) Use the  provided to form a pattern of 3 repeating units. You do not need to use all the shapes.

Chapter 13   Two-Dimensional and Three-Dimensional Figures

Put on Your Thinking Cap!

  Challenging Practice

The shapes at the bottom of this page can be combined to make a square.
Colour the pieces yellow.
Cut them out and paste them below to make the square.
You may also use the stickers at the back of the book.

Name: _____ Class: _____ Date: _____

CHAPTER 14 Fractions

Practice 1 Understanding Fractions

(1) Fill in the blanks.

Example

___1___ out of ___12___ equal parts is shaded.

___$\frac{1}{12}$___ of the figure is shaded.

(a)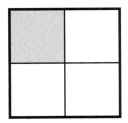

_____ out of _____ equal parts is shaded.

_____ of the figure is shaded.

(b)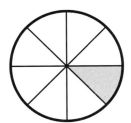

_____ out of _____ equal parts is shaded.

_____ of the figure is shaded.

Lesson 1 Understanding Fractions

(c)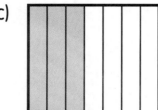

_3_ out of _7_ equal parts are shaded.

_3/7_ of the figure is shaded.

(d)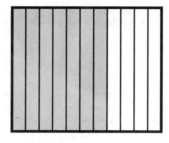

_7_ out of _11_ equal parts are shaded.

_7/11_ of the figure is shaded.

(e)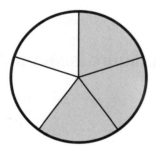

_3_ out of _5_ equal parts are shaded.

_3/5_ of the figure is shaded.

(f)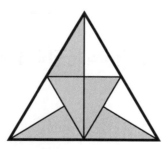

_5_ out of _8_ equal parts are shaded.

_5/8_ of the figure is shaded.

(2) Study the figures carefully.
Then, fill in the blanks.

(a)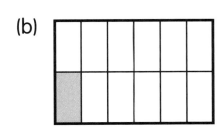

The circle is divided into
__6__ equal parts.
__1/6__ of the circle is shaded.

(b)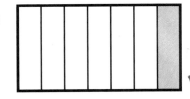

The rectangle is divided into
__12__ equal parts.
__1/12__ of the rectangle is shaded.

(3) What fraction of each figure is shaded?
Circle the answer.

(a)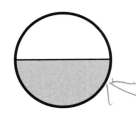

| $\frac{1}{6}$ | $\frac{1}{7}$ |

(b)

| $\frac{1}{2}$ | 1 |

(c)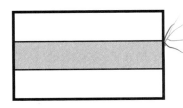

| $\frac{1}{2}$ | $\frac{1}{3}$ |

Lesson 1 Understanding Fractions

(4) Cross (X) the odd one out.

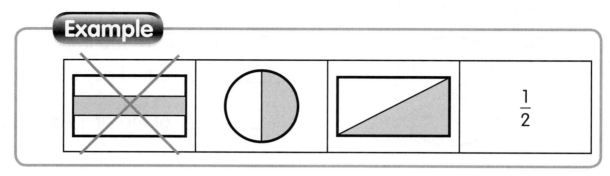

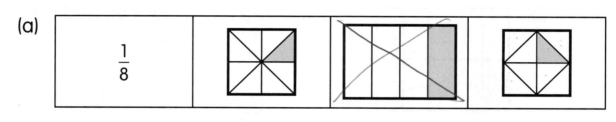

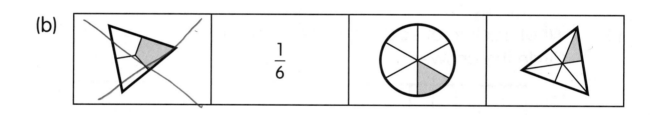

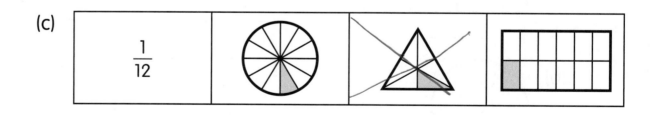

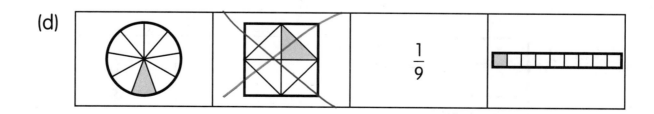

(5) What fraction of each figure is shaded?
Write the fraction in the box.

Example

(a)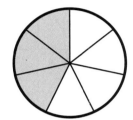

(b)

(c)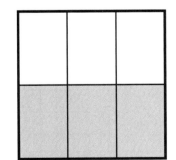

(d)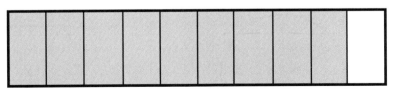

Lesson 1 Understanding Fractions

(6) Colour parts of each figure to show the fraction given.

Fraction	Figure 1	Figure 2
$\frac{2}{3}$		
$\frac{5}{8}$		
$\frac{2}{5}$		
$\frac{3}{10}$		
$\frac{5}{6}$		

(7) What fraction of each figure is **not** shaded?
Match the fractions to the figures.

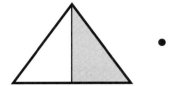 •

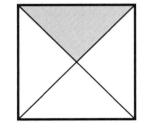 •

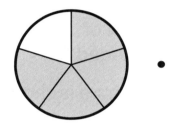 •

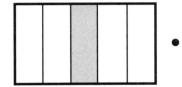 •

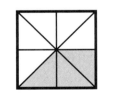 •

 •

• $\frac{2}{3}$

• $\frac{3}{4}$

• 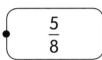 $\frac{1}{5}$

•  $\frac{5}{8}$

• $\frac{1}{4}$

• $\frac{1}{2}$

• $\frac{4}{5}$

• $\frac{1}{3}$

• $\frac{2}{5}$

• $\frac{3}{5}$

• $\frac{3}{8}$

Lesson 1 Understanding Fractions

(8) Each figure has been divided into equal parts.
Shade two or more parts of each figure.
Fill in the blanks.

Example

___3___ parts out of ___4___ equal parts are shaded.

___$\frac{3}{4}$___ of the figure is shaded.

___$\frac{1}{4}$___ of the figure is not shaded.

(a)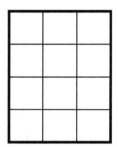

_____ parts out of _____ equal parts are shaded.

_____ of the figure is shaded

_____ of the figure is not shaded.

(b)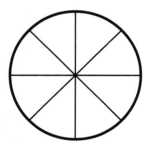

_____ parts out of _____ equal parts are shaded.

_____ of the figure is shaded.

_____ of the figure is not shaded.

(c)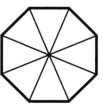

_____ parts out of _____ equal parts are shaded.

_____ of the figure is shaded.

_____ of the figure is not shaded.

Chapter 14 Fractions

Practice 2 More Fractions

(1) Fill in the blanks.

| $\frac{1}{3}$ | $\frac{1}{3}$ | $\frac{1}{3}$ |

_____ of the whole is unshaded.

_____ of the whole is shaded.

$\frac{2}{3}$ is _____ out of _____ equal parts.

$\frac{2}{3}$ = _____ + _____

(2) A pizza is cut into 7 equal slices.
Andy eats 4 slices.

_____ slices are left.

The fraction of the pizza eaten by Andy is _____.

The fraction of the pizza left is _____.

_____ and _____ make 1 whole.

(3) A chocolate bar has 8 equal parts.
Sam eats 5 parts.

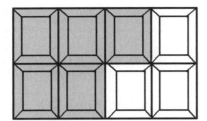

_____ parts are left.

The fraction of the chocolate eaten by Sam is _____.

The fraction of the chocolate left is _____.

_____ and _____ make 1 whole.

(4) Find the fractions.

(a) _____ and $\frac{6}{8}$ make 1 whole.

(b) $\frac{3}{10}$ and _____ make 1 whole.

(c) _____ and $\frac{6}{12}$ make 1 whole.

(d) $\frac{6}{11}$ and _____ make 1 whole.

Practice 3 Comparing and Ordering Fractions

(1) Colour the following fractions.

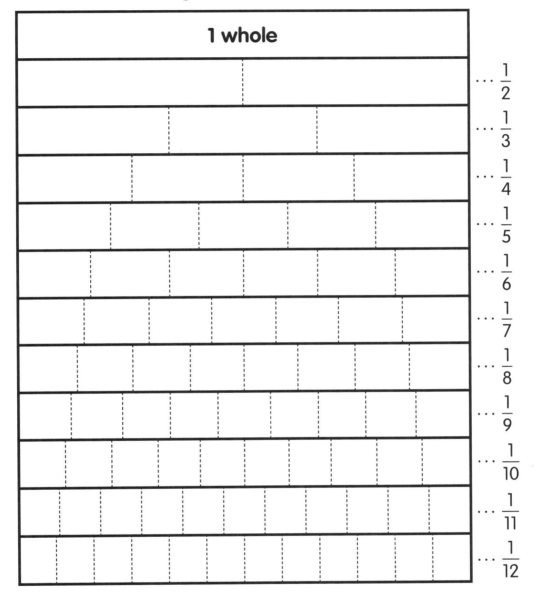

(a) Which of these fractions is the greatest? _____

(b) Which of these fractions is the smallest? _____

(c) Order the fractions from smallest to greatest.

___, ___, ___, ___, ___, ___, ___, ___, ___, ___, ___
smallest

(2) Write the fraction of the shaded part.
Then, compare the fractions.

Example

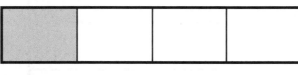

__$\frac{1}{4}$__ is shaded.

__$\frac{1}{3}$__ is shaded.

__$\frac{1}{3}$__ is greater than __$\frac{1}{4}$__.

__$\frac{1}{4}$__ is smaller than __$\frac{1}{3}$__.

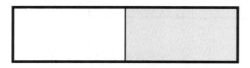

_____ is shaded.

_____ is shaded.

_____ is greater than _____.

_____ is smaller than _____.

Chapter 14 Fractions

(3) Look at the figures.
Circle the greater fraction.

(a)  $\frac{1}{2}$

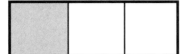 $\frac{1}{3}$

(b) 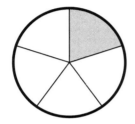 $\frac{1}{5}$  $\frac{1}{6}$

(4) Look at the figures.
Circle the smaller fraction.

(a) 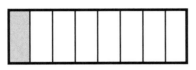 $\frac{1}{8}$

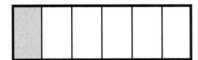 $\frac{1}{6}$

(b) 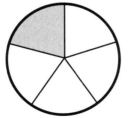 $\frac{1}{5}$ 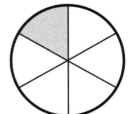 $\frac{1}{6}$

Lesson 3 Comparing and Ordering Fractions

(5) Circle the greater fraction.

(a) $\dfrac{1}{6}$ $\dfrac{1}{8}$ (b) $\dfrac{1}{5}$ $\dfrac{1}{9}$

(6) Circle the smaller fraction.

(a) $\dfrac{1}{4}$ $\dfrac{1}{5}$ (b) $\dfrac{1}{9}$ $\dfrac{1}{6}$

(7) Najib is given sets of fractions.
Help him to arrange the fractions in order.

(a) Begin with the greatest.

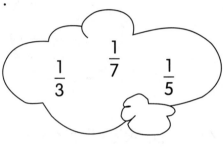

_____, _____, _____
greatest

(b) Begin with the smallest.

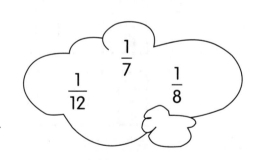

_____, _____, _____
smallest

(c) Begin with the greatest.

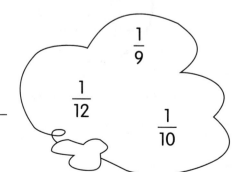

_____, _____, _____
greatest

Chapter 14 Fractions

(8) Three students were each given a loaf of bread.

Junwen ate $\frac{5}{9}$ of a loaf of bread.

Lynn ate $\frac{4}{9}$ of a loaf of bread.

Jai ate $\frac{8}{9}$ of a loaf of bread.

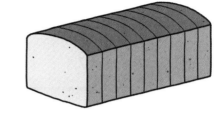

Colour to show the amount of bread each of them ate.

Junwen $\frac{5}{9}$

Lynn $\frac{4}{9}$

Jai $\frac{8}{9}$

$\frac{5}{9}$ is greater than _____.

Junwen ate more than _____.

_____ ate the most.

_____ ate the least.

(9) (a) What fraction of each figure is shaded? Circle the greater fraction.

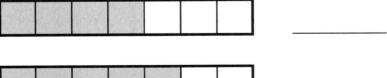

(b) Fill in the blanks with the above fractions.

_____ is smaller than _____.

Lesson 3   Comparing and Ordering Fractions

(10) Circle the smaller fraction.

(a) $\frac{3}{7}$ $\frac{5}{7}$ (b) $\frac{2}{9}$ $\frac{7}{9}$

(11) Circle the greater fraction.

(a) $\frac{3}{8}$ $\frac{5}{8}$ (b) $\frac{5}{11}$ $\frac{10}{11}$

(12) (a) Look at the figures.
Circle the greatest fraction.

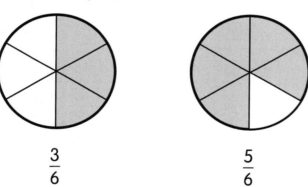

$\frac{3}{6}$ $\frac{5}{6}$ $\frac{1}{6}$

(b) Look at the figures.
Circle the smallest fraction.

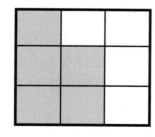 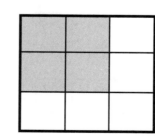 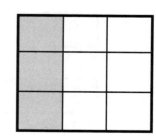

$\frac{5}{9}$ $\frac{4}{9}$ $\frac{3}{9}$

Chapter 14   Fractions

(13) Circle the greatest fraction.

(a) $\frac{3}{10}$ $\frac{1}{10}$ $\frac{9}{10}$ (b) $\frac{1}{6}$ $\frac{4}{6}$ $\frac{2}{6}$

(14) Circle the smallest fraction.

(a) $\frac{3}{8}$ $\frac{5}{8}$ $\frac{2}{8}$ (b) $\frac{6}{7}$ $\frac{4}{7}$ $\frac{3}{7}$

(15) Arrange each set of fractions in order.

  (a) Begin with the greatest.

    $\frac{3}{8}, \frac{7}{8}, \frac{5}{8}$

    _____, _____, _____
    greatest

  (b) Begin with the smallest.

    $\frac{8}{10}, \frac{4}{10}, \frac{7}{10}$

    _____, _____, _____
    smallest

Lesson 3   Comparing and Ordering Fractions

(16) Shade the strips to show the fractions.
Then, fill in the blanks using these fractions.

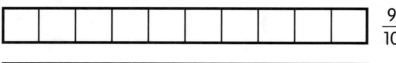 $\dfrac{3}{10}$

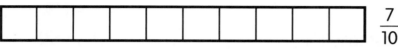 $\dfrac{9}{10}$

$\dfrac{7}{10}$

_____ is greater than _____.

_____ is smaller than _____.

The greatest fraction is _____.

The smallest fraction is _____.

(17) Shade the figures to show the fractions.
Then, fill in the blanks using these fractions.

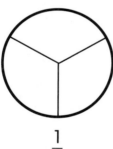 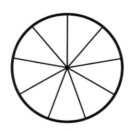 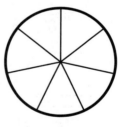

$\dfrac{1}{3}$ $\dfrac{1}{9}$ $\dfrac{1}{7}$

_____ is greater than _____.

_____ is smaller than _____.

The greatest fraction is _____.

The smallest fraction is _____.

Practice 4 Addition and Subtraction of Like Fractions

(1) Write the correct fraction in each box.
Use the pictures to help you.

(a) Add $\frac{1}{5}$ and $\frac{2}{5}$.

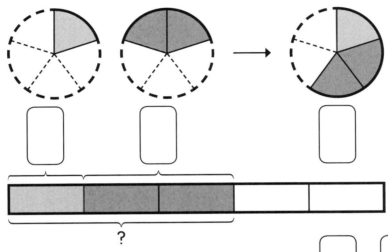

(b) Add $\frac{1}{6}$ and $\frac{2}{6}$.

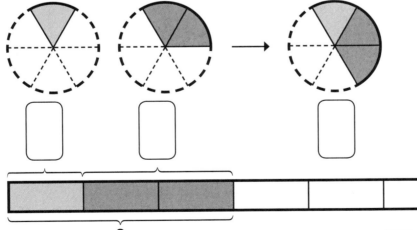

Lesson 4 Addition and Subtraction of Like Fractions

(2) Write the correct fraction in each box.

(a)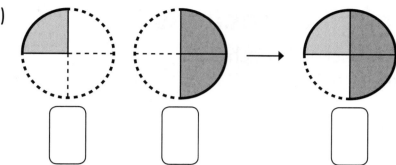

(b)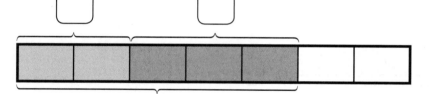

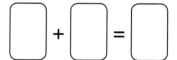

(c)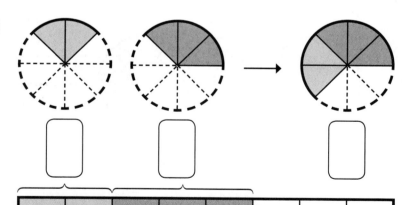

(d)

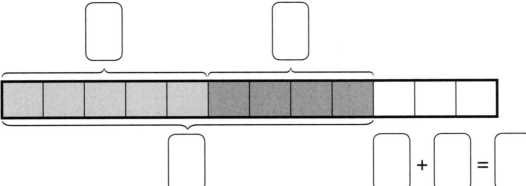

(3) Add.

(a) $\frac{1}{3} + \frac{1}{3} =$ _____

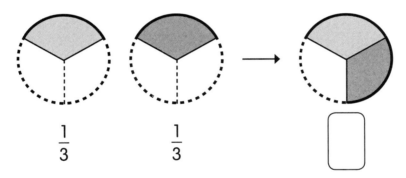

(b) $\frac{1}{4} + \frac{2}{4} =$ _____

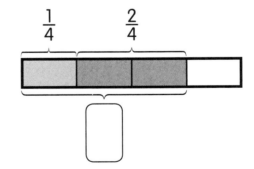

(c) $\frac{1}{2} + \frac{1}{2} =$ _____

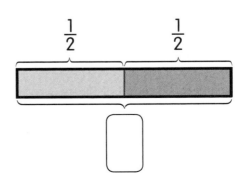

Lesson 4 Addition and Subtraction of Like Fractions

(4) Add.

(a) $\frac{1}{4} + \frac{2}{4}$ = _____

(b) $\frac{2}{5} + \frac{1}{5}$ = _____

(c) $\frac{2}{5} + \frac{2}{5}$ = _____

(d) $\frac{3}{7} + \frac{1}{7}$ = _____

(e) $\frac{2}{9} + \frac{3}{9}$ = _____

(f) $\frac{5}{11} + \frac{4}{11}$ = _____

(g) $\frac{1}{2} + \frac{1}{2}$ = _____

(h) $\frac{1}{4} + \frac{3}{4}$ = _____

(i) $\frac{1}{6} + \frac{3}{6}$ = _____

(j) $\frac{4}{8} + \frac{3}{8}$ = _____

(k) $\frac{3}{10} + \frac{4}{10}$ = _____

(l) $\frac{5}{12} + \frac{4}{12}$ = _____

(5) Write the correct fraction in each box.

(a) Subtract $\frac{5}{8}$ from 1.

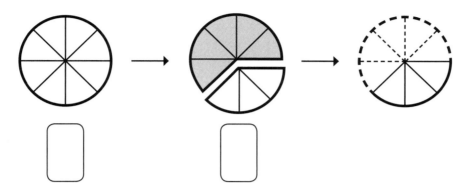

(b) Subtract $\frac{6}{10}$ from 1.

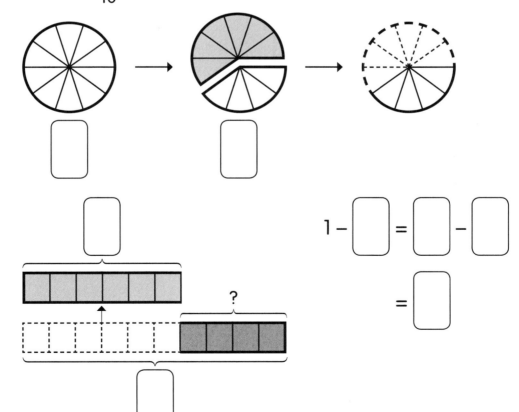

Lesson 4 Addition and Subtraction of Like Fractions

(6) Write the correct fraction in each box.

(a)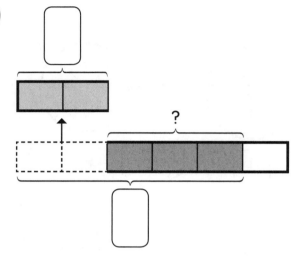

(b)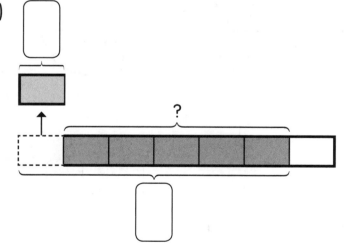

3/3

(7) Subtract.

(a) $1 - \frac{2}{3} = \dfrac{1}{3}$

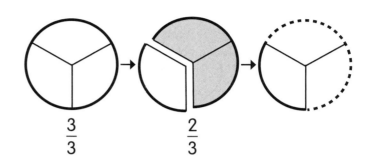

(b) $\frac{3}{4} - \frac{2}{4} = \dfrac{1}{4}$

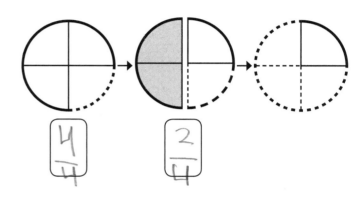

$\dfrac{4}{4}$ $\dfrac{2}{4}$

(c) $\frac{3}{4} - \frac{1}{4} = \dfrac{2}{4}$

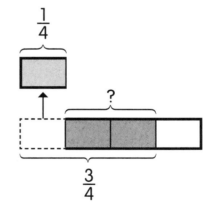

(d) $\frac{2}{3} - \frac{1}{3} = \dfrac{1}{3}$

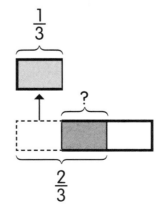

Lesson 4 Addition and Subtraction of Like Fractions

(8) Subtract.

(a) $\frac{4}{5} - \frac{1}{5} = \frac{3}{5}$

(b) $\frac{5}{6} - \frac{4}{6} = \frac{1}{6}$

(c) $\frac{6}{8} - \frac{3}{8} = \frac{3}{8}$

(d) $\frac{9}{11} - \frac{3}{11} = \frac{6}{11}$

(e) $\frac{6}{7} - \frac{3}{7} = \frac{3}{7}$

(f) $\frac{11}{12} - \frac{4}{12} = \frac{7}{12}$

(g) $\frac{7}{10} - \frac{4}{10} = \frac{3}{10}$

(h) $\frac{7}{8} - \frac{3}{8} = \frac{4}{8}$

(i) $1 - \frac{7}{9} = \frac{2}{9}$
$\frac{9}{9} - \frac{7}{9}$

(j) $1 - \frac{5}{10} = \frac{5}{10}$
$\frac{10}{10}$

(k) $\frac{8}{12} - \frac{2}{12} = \frac{6}{12}$

(l) $\frac{9}{12} - \frac{5}{12} = \frac{4}{12}$

Name: _____ Class: _____ Date: _____

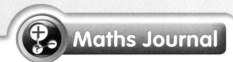

Will Mariam get more of the ice cream?

Use diagrams to show your answer.

Name: _____ Class: _____ Date: _____

 **Performance Task**

You are given 3 shapes.

Shade $\frac{1}{2}$ of each shape and paste them here.

Are the halves the same?

Chapter 14 Fractions

Put on Your Thinking Cap!

  Challenging Practice

(1) How many more parts must be shaded to show $\frac{3}{4}$? _____

(2) What fraction of each strip is shaded?

Order the fractions from greatest to smallest.

_____, _____, _____
greatest

(3) Charlie drew two figures, A and B.
Part of A is covered by an ink blob.

By comparing A and B, what fraction of A is **not** covered by the ink blob? _____

Chapter 14 Fractions

Put on Your Thinking Cap!

 Problem Solving

Meijun is at a fractions party.
Help her cross out all fractions greater than $\frac{1}{8}$.
Circle the remaining balloon.

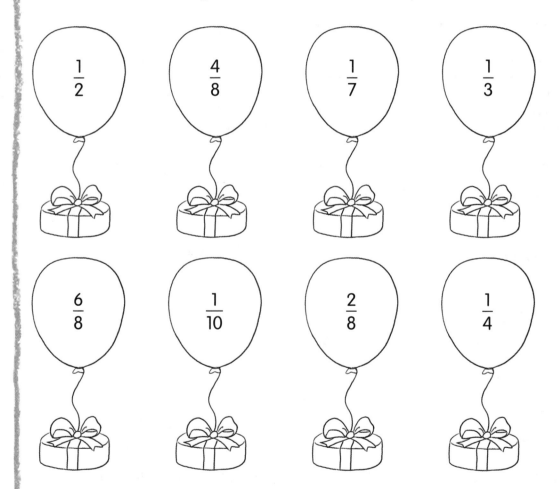

Name: _____ Class: _____ Date: _____

Review 5

(1) Circle the shapes with curves only.

(2) Copy this figure to the dot grid on the right.

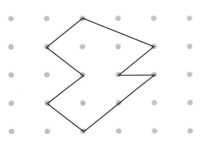

(3) Copy this figure to the square grid on the right.

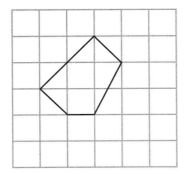 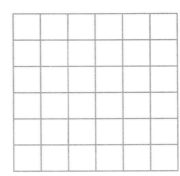

Review 5 | 129

(4) Each of the figures is made up of shapes.
Name the shapes.

(a) This figure is made up of _____,

_____ and _____.

(b) This figure is made up of _____,

_____ and _____.

(5) (a) Fill in the blanks.
Use the words in the box.

| Sphere | Cuboid | Cylinder |

A
_____

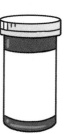
B
_____

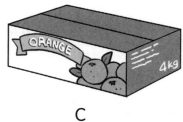
C
_____

(b) Which object has no flat surfaces? _____

Review 5

(6) Colour the solids used in the figure.

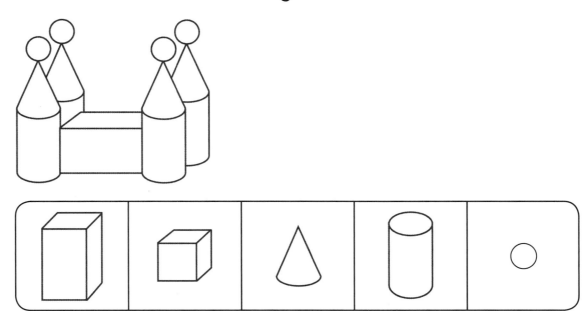

(7) Look at the pattern.
Circle what comes next.

(a) △ ○ □ △ ○ □ △ ○ □ △ ○ [△/□]

(b) ▭ ○ ▭ ● ▭ ○ ▭ ● ▭ ○ ▭ ● ▭ ○ [▭/●]

(8) Look at the pattern.
Circle what comes next.

(a) ○ ▯ △ ▯ ○ ▯ △ ▯ ○ ▯ △ ▯ [○/△]

(b) ▯ ▭ ▭ ▯ ▯ ▭ ▭ ▯ ▯ ▭ ▭ ▯ [▯/▭]

Review 5

(9) Which of the following shows $\frac{1}{3}$ shaded? Tick (✓) the correct figures.

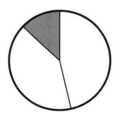   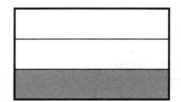

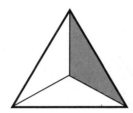   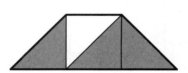

(10) Fill in the blanks.

(a)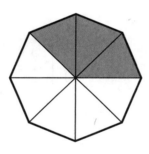

The figure is divided into __8__ equal parts.

__3__ parts of the figure are shaded.

__$\frac{3}{8}$__ of the figure is shaded.

(b)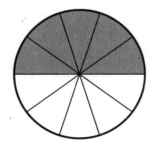

The circle is divided into __10__ equal parts.

__5__ parts of the circle are shaded.

__$\frac{5}{10}$__ of the figure is shaded.

Review 5

(11) Shade each figure to show the fraction.

(a)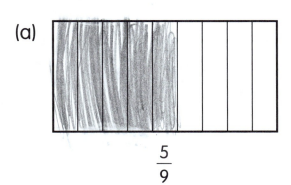

$\frac{5}{9}$

(b)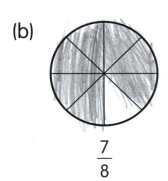

$\frac{7}{8}$

(12) Colour $\frac{2}{7}$ of the figure red.

Colour $\frac{3}{7}$ of the figure green.

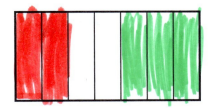

What fraction of the figure is coloured? $\frac{5}{7}$

What fraction of the figure is not coloured? $\frac{2}{7}$

(13) (a) Shade the strips.
Order the fractions from greatest to smallest.

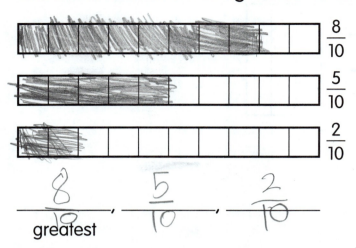

$\dfrac{8}{10}$, $\dfrac{5}{10}$, $\dfrac{2}{10}$
greatest

(b) Two of these fractions make 1 whole. What are they?

$\dfrac{8}{10}$ and $\dfrac{2}{10}$

(14) Shade the strips.
Order the fractions from greatest to smallest.

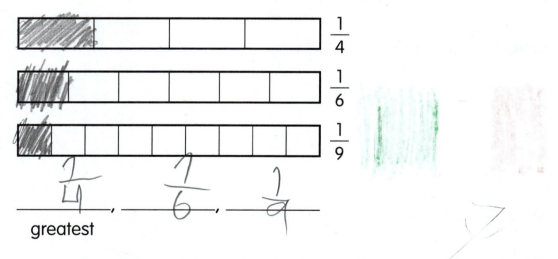

$\dfrac{1}{4}$, $\dfrac{1}{6}$, $\dfrac{1}{9}$
greatest

(15) Order the fractions from smallest to greatest.

$\dfrac{1}{10}$, $\dfrac{1}{7}$, $\dfrac{1}{12}$

$\dfrac{1}{12}$, $\dfrac{1}{7}$, $\dfrac{1}{10}$
smallest

Review 5

(16) What fraction of each strip is coloured?
Fill in the blanks.

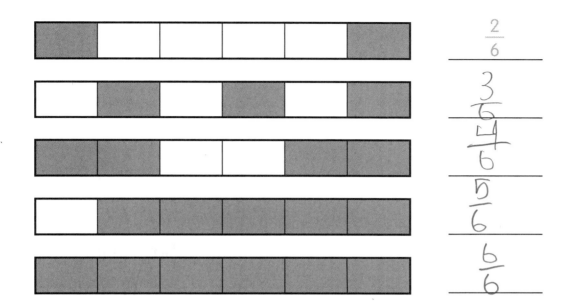

$\frac{2}{6}$

$\frac{3}{6}$

$\frac{4}{6}$

$\frac{5}{6}$

$\frac{6}{6}$

Use your answers above to fill in the blanks.

(a) $\frac{3}{6}$ is greater than _____.

(b) $\frac{4}{6}$ is smaller than _____.

(c) _____ is the smallest fraction.

(d) _____ is the greatest fraction.

(17) (a) Add $\frac{2}{3}$ and $\frac{1}{3}$.

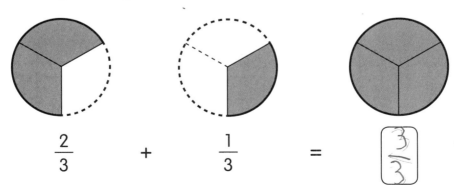

$\frac{2}{3}$ + $\frac{1}{3}$ = $\boxed{\frac{3}{3}}$

Review 5

(b) Subtract $\frac{2}{6}$ from $\frac{5}{6}$.

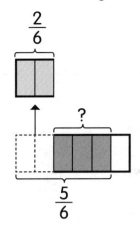

$\frac{5}{6} - \frac{2}{6} = \boxed{}$

(18) Add or subtract the fractions.

(a) $\frac{3}{8} + \frac{2}{8} =$ _____

(b) $\frac{4}{10} + \frac{3}{10} =$ _____

(c) $\frac{3}{7} + \frac{3}{7} =$ _____

(d) $\frac{4}{9} + \frac{5}{9} =$ _____

(e) $\frac{7}{9} - \frac{5}{9} =$ _____

(f) $\frac{5}{8} - \frac{4}{8} =$ _____

(g) $\frac{11}{12} - \frac{6}{12} =$ _____

(h) $1 - \frac{7}{10} =$ _____

Time

Practice 1 Reading and Writing Time

(1) Fill in the blanks with the number of minutes.

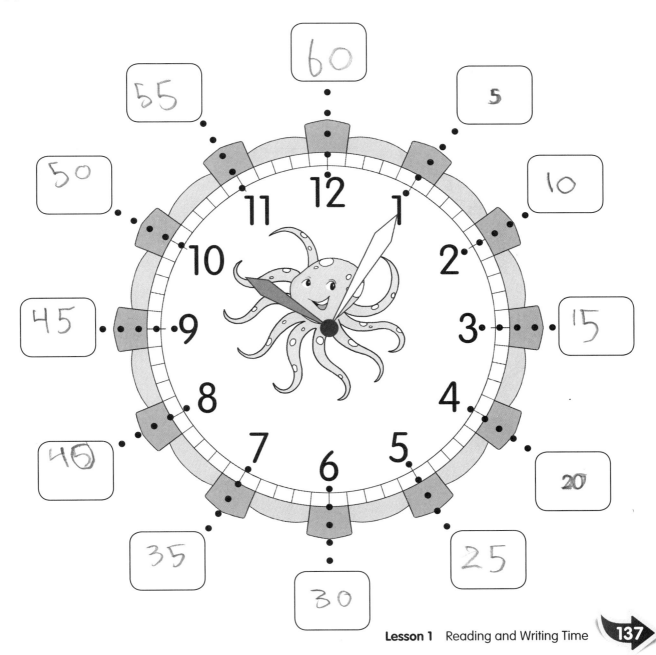

(2) Fill in the blanks.

Example

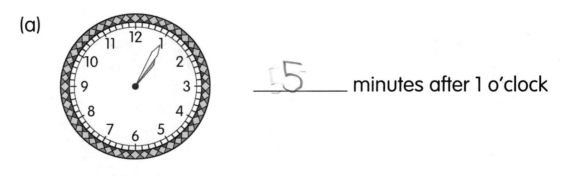

_____30_____ minutes after 9 o'clock

(a)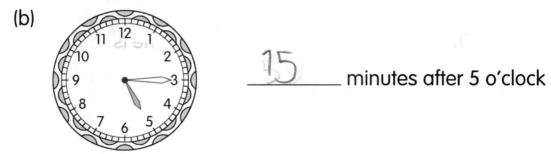

_____5_____ minutes after 1 o'clock

(b)

_____15_____ minutes after 5 o'clock

(c)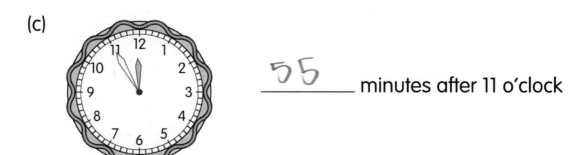

_____55_____ minutes after 11 o'clock

(3) Fill in the blanks with the correct time.

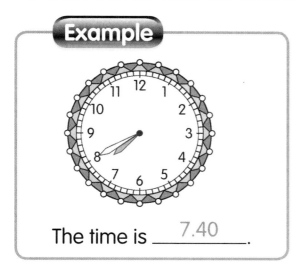

Example

The time is ___7.40___.

(a) The time is ___5:45___.

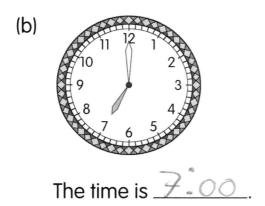

(b) The time is ___7:00___.

(c) The time is ___12:26___.

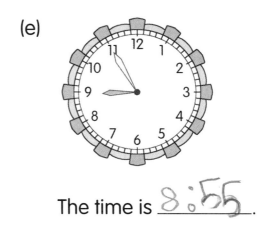

(d) The time is ___6:05___.

(e) The time is ___8:55___.

Lesson 1 Reading and Writing Time

(4) Draw the minute hand to show the time.
　　(a)　4.15　　　　　　　　　　(b)　6.40

　　(c)　3.45　　　　　　　　　　(d)　10.35

Practice 2 Learning a.m. and p.m.

Fill in the blanks with **a.m.** or **p.m.**

Example

Sam has breakfast at 6.30 ___a.m.___

(1)

(a) Sam's family wakes up early to exercise at the park every weekend at 6.50 ___a.m___

(b) Sam loves to read storybooks in the afternoon at 2.50 ___a.m___

(c) At 6.30 __p.m.__, Sam has dinner with his family.

(d) The sun sets at about 7.25 __p.m.__

(e) Sam's father likes to go jogging at night. He usually jogs at 8.30 __p.m.__

(2)

(a) Xiuzhen woke up at 7.30 __a.m.__

(b) Xiuzhen and her mother left for the grocery store at 9.30 __a.m.__

(c) Xiuzhen and her mother paid for their groceries at 10.30 __a.m.__

(d) They reached home from the grocery store at 11.00 __a.m.__

(e) Xiuzhen helped her mother put away the groceries. Then, they started preparing lunch at 11.30 __a.m.__

12:00 noon

(f) The family had lunch at 12.30 __p.m.__

Chapter 15 Time

Name: Jimena   Class: 2.3   Date: 5\6

Practice 3   Time Taken in Hours and Minutes

(1) Fill in the blanks with the correct times.

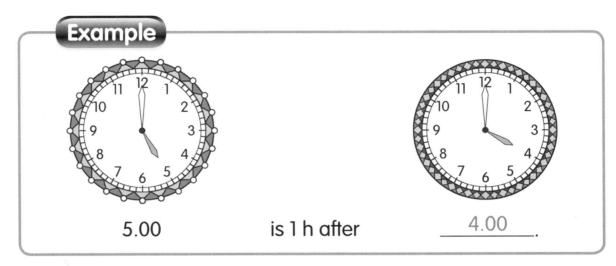

Example

5.00 is 1 h after ___4.00___.

(a)

12.00 is 1 h after ___11:00___.

(b)

8.00 is 1 h after ___7:00___.

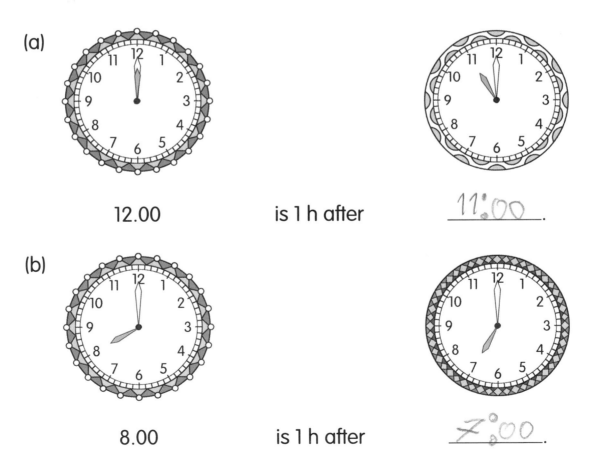

Lesson 3   Time Taken in Hours and Minutes   145

(c)

11.00   is 1 h after   __10:00__.

(d)

__5:00__   is half an hour after   4.30.

(e)

__1:30__   is half an hour after   1.00.

(2) Fill in the blanks with the correct times.

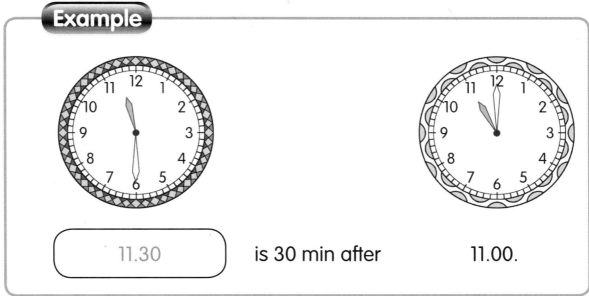

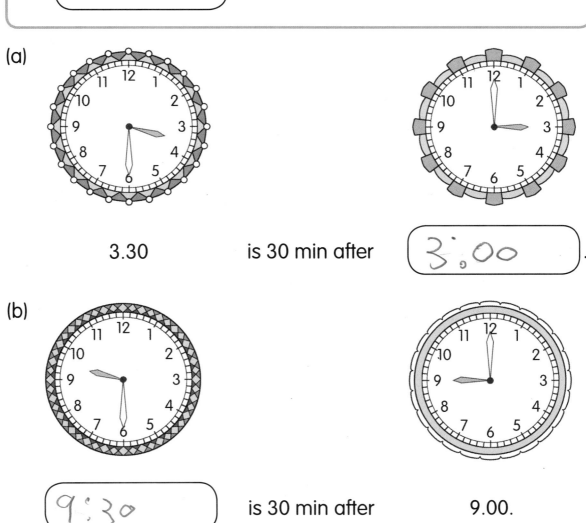

(c)

7.00   is 30 min after   6.30 .

*(3) Draw the hands on each clock and write the time.

(a)

12:30   is half an hour after   12:00 .

(b)

2:00   is 1 h after   1:00 .

(4) Fill in the blanks with the number of minutes or hours.

(a) Captain James left his ship at 8.00 a.m. and arrived on shore at 8.30 a.m.

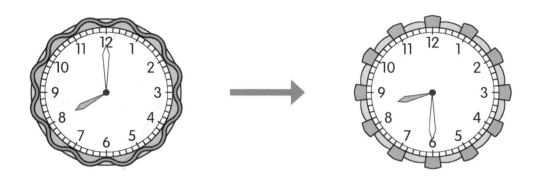

He took __30__ minutes.

(b) Peter played basketball from 6.00 p.m. to 7.00 p.m.

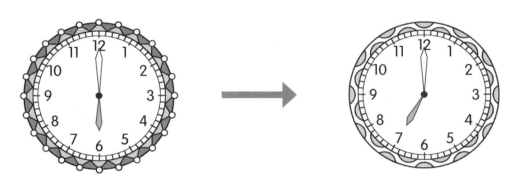

He played for __1__ hour.

Lesson 3 Time Taken in Hours and Minutes

Name: Jineva   Class: 2.3   Date: 6/6

Maths Journal

Find the mistakes and correct them.

(1)

Pamela wrote: The time is 4.25.

The correct time is __5:25__.

(2) Banu drew the hands on the clock to show 7.55.
This is how she did it.

The correct way of drawing is .

Chapter 15   Time

Performance Task

(1) Use  to show the times below.
Then, draw the times.

Time	Draw the Hands
8.20	
1.50	

(2) Your teacher will show a time on .
Write down the times he or she shows.

(a) 7:15

(b) 2:40

(c) 6:30

(3) Look at the TV programme list.

TV Programme List

Channel 3	Monday
7.30 a.m.	Morning Live!
8.30 a.m.	A.M. News
9.30 a.m.	Let's Get Healthy
11.30 a.m.	Asian Food Delights
12.00 noon	Sands of Time
1.00 p.m.	Sports News
3.00 p.m.	Karaoke Battle
4.00 p.m.	Science Challenge
4.30 p.m.	Math Attack
5.00 p.m.	Animals Around the World
6.00 p.m.	Art for Kids
6.30 p.m.	Crazy Cartoons
7.00 p.m.	The New World
9.30 p.m.	The Nightly News
10.00 p.m.	Movie Special: The Toys
12.00 midnight	End

(a) Write down the title of a programme that is 1 hour long.

_____

(b) Write down the title of a programme that is half an hour long.

_____

Put on Your Thinking Cap!

  Challenging Practice

Penny's father started jogging at 8.00 a.m.
He jogged for an hour.
Draw the hands on the clock to show the time he finished jogging.

Penny finished jogging at 15 minutes after 9.00 a.m.
Draw the hands on the clock to show the time she finished jogging.

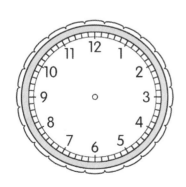 

Who finished jogging later? _____

Chapter 15 Time

Name: _____ Class: _____ Date: _____

 Put on Your Thinking Cap!

 Problem Solving

Draw the hands on the clocks to show the times.

Othman started his homework at 6.00 p.m.

1 h later

He spent 1 hour writing his story.

30 min later

He took another 30 minutes to colour the pictures.

Othman finished his homework at _____.

154 Chapter 15 Time

Name: _____ Class: _____ Date: _____

Chapter 16 Picture Graphs

Practice 1 Reading Picture Graphs with Scales

(1) After a walk, Jack and his friends were very hungry.
The picture graph shows the amount of food they ate.

Amount of Food Eaten

Each 🍱 stands for 2 servings of food.

(a) They had _____ servings of *roti prata*.

(b) They had the same number of servings of _____ as *roti prata*.

(c) They had _____ more servings of noodles than *nasi lemak*.

(d) They had _____ servings of noodles and *nasi lemak* altogether.

*(e) Each serving of pie cost $4.
The pies they ate cost $_____ altogether.

(2) Jane and her classmates are telling one another about their favourite fairy tale characters.
This picture graph shows their choices.

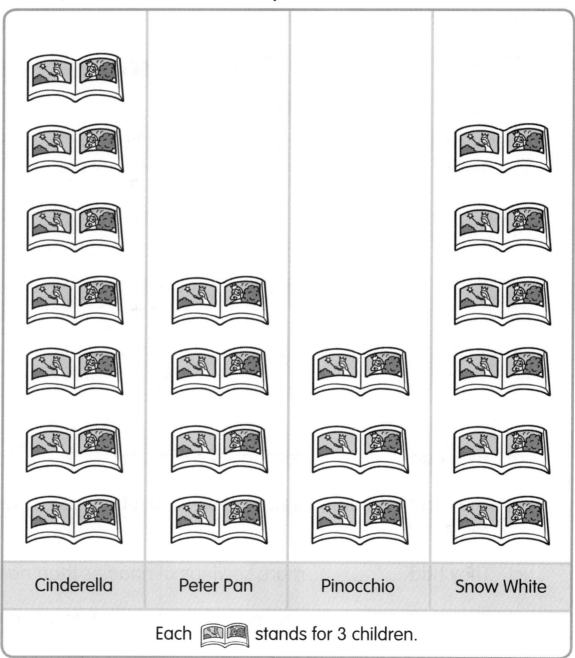

Favourite Fairy Tale Characters

Each 📖 stands for 3 children.

(a) How many fairy tale characters are shown?

_____

(b) Which is the most popular fairy tale character?

_____

(c) Which is the least popular fairy tale character?

_____

(d) How many children choose Peter Pan as their favourite character?

_____

(e) How many children choose Cinderella as their favourite character?

_____

(f) How many more children choose Snow White over Peter Pan as their favourite character?

_____

(g) How many children choose Peter Pan or Pinocchio as their favourite characters altogether?

_____

(3) Fandi's school has a canteen, a hall, a general office and an AVA room.
He draws a picture graph to show how far his classroom is from these places.

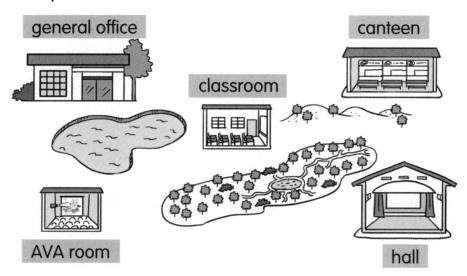

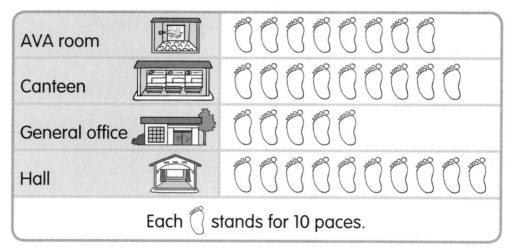

(a) The hall is _____ paces from Fandi's classroom.

(b) The canteen is _____ paces from Fandi's classroom.

(c) Fandi's classroom is _____ paces from the general office.

(d) The AVA room is _____ more paces from Fandi's classroom than the general office.

(4) The picture graph shows the number of children playing at each game stall at a funfair.

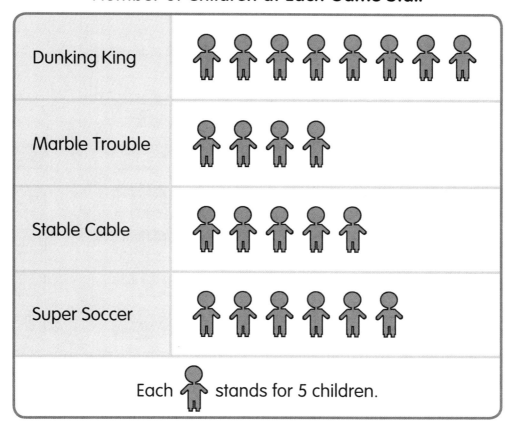

(a) Which is the most popular game stall? _____

(b) How many children are at the Stable Cable stall? _____

(c) 5 of the children who play at the Dunking King stall are girls.
How many of them are boys? _____

(5) The picture graph shows the number of people who went to the cinema on Sunday.

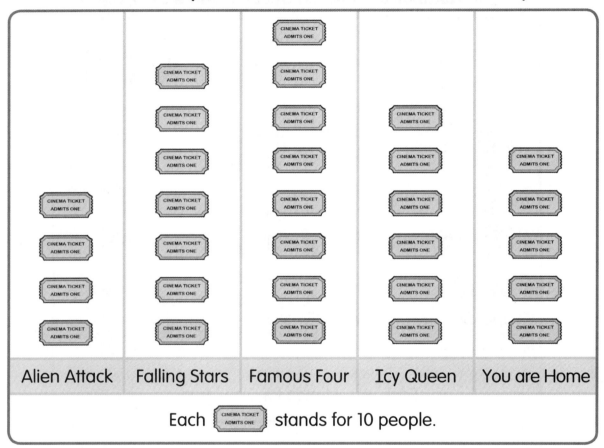

(a) 60 men watched Falling Stars.
How many women watched Falling Stars? _____

(b) 60 women watched Icy Queen.
How many men watched Icy Queen? _____

(c) How many people watched Alien Attack and You are Home altogether? _____

*(6) Rila and her friends are comparing their pencil collections. She draws a picture graph to show the number of pencils they have. However, she accidentally spills her drink on parts of the picture graph.

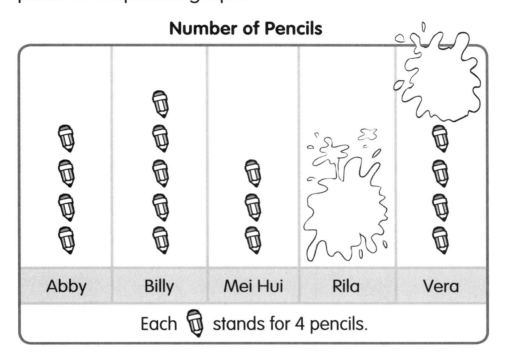

(a) How many pencils does Abby have? _____

(b) How many more pencils does Billy have than Mei Hui?

_____

(c) Rila has 8 pencils.
How many 🖉 should there be on the graph? _____

(d) Vera has 24 pencils.
How many more 🖉 must there be on the graph? _____

(e) How many pencils do Abby and Mei Hui have altogether? _____

Lesson 1   Reading Picture Graphs with Scales

Name: _____ Class: _____ Date: _____

Maths Journal

Valerie is baking banana cupcakes for her family.
Write four sentences about the picture graph.

Ingredients for Banana Cupcakes

Butter	△		
Mashed bananas	△	△	△
Milk	△	△	
Oat cereal	△	△	△
Sugar	△		

Each △ stands for 2 cups.

Example

She uses 4 cups of milk.

_____

_____

_____

_____

162   Chapter 16   Picture Graphs

Name: _____ Class: _____ Date: _____

Performance Task

Dr Lee saw a total of 45 patients today.
15 of them were girls and the rest were boys.

Use  to make a picture graph to show the number of boys and girls who consulted Dr Lee today.

Dr Lee's Patients Today

Boys	Girls

Each 📷 stands for 5 patients.

Chapter 16 Picture Graphs

Name: _____ Class: _____ Date: _____

Challenging Practice

Peiling records the number of eggs she picks from her chicken farm every day for 3 days.

The picture graph shows the number of eggs she picks from her chicken farm.
The number of eggs Peiling picks follows a pattern.

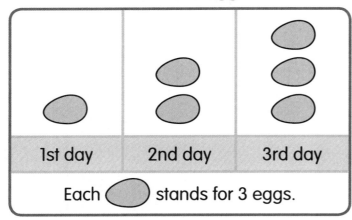

If this pattern carries on,

(a) how many eggs will Peiling pick on the 4th day?

Peiling will pick _____ eggs on the 4th day.

(b) how many eggs will Peiling pick on the 5th day?

Peiling will pick _____ eggs on the 5th day.

(c) how many eggs will Peiling pick on the 7th day?

Peiling will pick _____ eggs on the 7th day.

# Put on Your Thinking Cap!

 ## Problem Solving

The picture graph shows the marks five children scored for their Mathematics test.
The total score for the test was 40.

Complete the picture graph using the data given.

> Madeline scored 28 marks.
> Wayne scored full marks.
> Fahmi scored 8 marks fewer than Wayne.
> Yuying and Shanti had the same score.

Marks Scored in the Mathematics Test

Each ⭐ stands for 4 marks.

Chapter 16 Picture Graphs

Name: _____ Class: _____ Date: _____

CHAPTER 17 Volume

Practice 1 Getting to Know Volume

Fill in the blanks with **more**, **less** or **same**.

(1)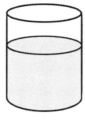
   A   B

The containers have the same size.

(a) Container B has _____ water than Container A.

(b) Container A has _____ water than Container B.

(2)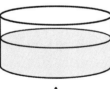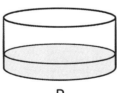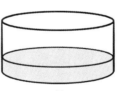
   A   B   C

The containers have the same size.

(a) Container A has _____ water than Container B.

(b) Container B has _____ water than Container A.

(c) Container B has the _____ amount of water as Container C.

Lesson 1 Getting to Know Volume 167

Fill in the blanks.

(3)

  A   B   C   D

The containers have the same size.

(a) Container _____ has the most amount of water.

(b) Container _____ has the least amount of water.

(4)

  A   B   C   D

The containers do not have the same size.

(a) Container _____ has the most amount of water.

(b) Container _____ has the least amount of water.

(5)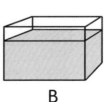

  A   B   C

The containers do not have the same size.

(a) Container _____ has the most amount of water.

(b) Container _____ has the least amount of water.

Chapter 17 Volume

(6) Water is scooped out of a pail and poured into these containers. Each ⬜ is one scoop.

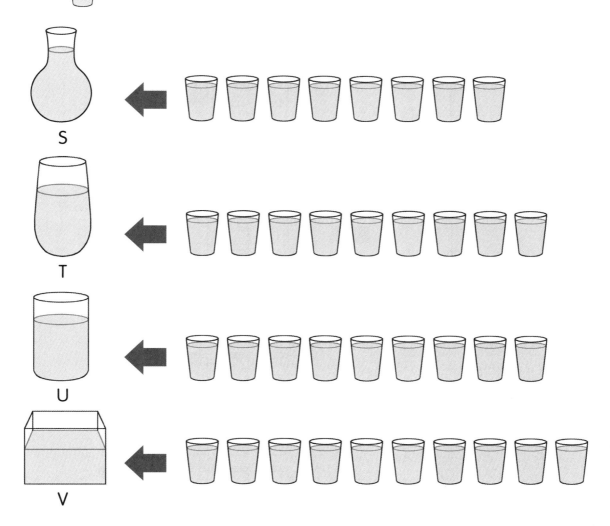

(a) Container _____ has the most amount of water.

(b) Container _____ has the least amount of water.

(c) Containers _____ and _____ have the same amount of water.

(d) Container _____ has more water than Container U.

(e) Container T has less water than Container _____.

(7) All the water in each fish tank is used to fill the glasses.

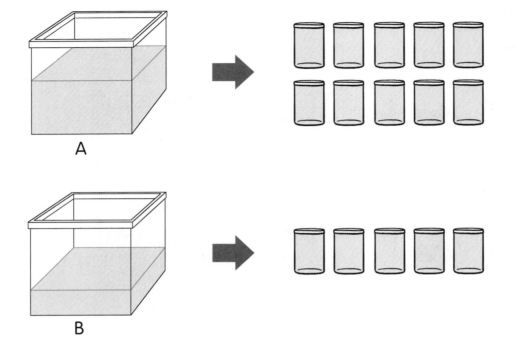

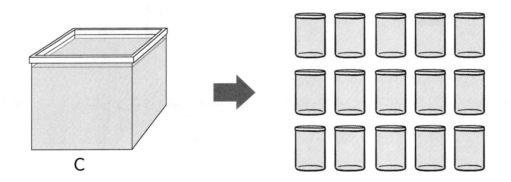

(a) Which fish tank has the most amount of water? _____

(b) Which fish tank has the least amount of water? _____

(c) Which fish tank has a smaller amount of water,
Fish tank A or Fish tank B? _____

Practice 2   Measuring in Litres

(1)   Fill in the blanks with **more than** or **less than**.

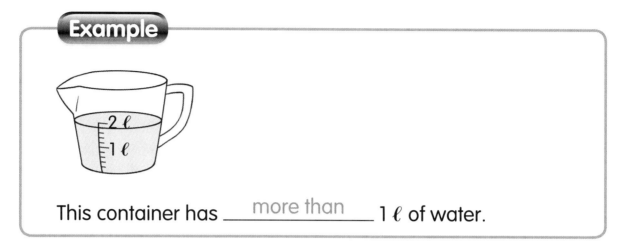

This container has ____more than____ 1 ℓ of water.

(a)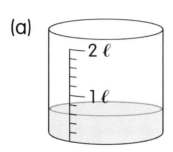

This container has _____ 1 ℓ of water.

(b)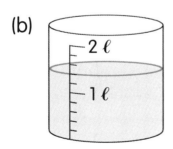

This container has _____ 1 ℓ of water.

(2) Fill in the blanks.
What is the volume of liquid in each container?

(a)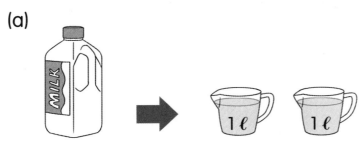

Dad pours _____ ℓ of milk for the family.

(b)

Mother makes _____ ℓ of tea for a tea party.

(c)

The office workers drink _____ ℓ of water every day.

(3) Susan uses different types of juices to make fruit punch.

orange juice 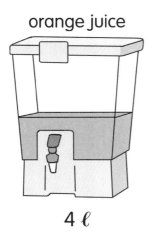 grape juice 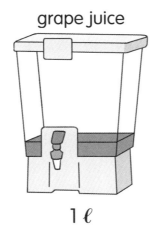 apple juice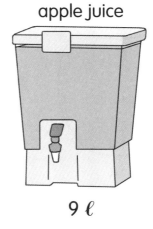

4 ℓ   1 ℓ   9 ℓ

(a) Susan uses more _____ juice than orange juice.

(b) Susan uses _____ ℓ more apple juice than grape juice.

(c) Susan uses _____ ℓ more apple juice than orange juice.

(d) Arrange the amounts of juices, in litres, from least to greatest.

_____ , _____ , _____
    least

Lesson 2   Measuring in Litres

(4) Fill in the blanks.

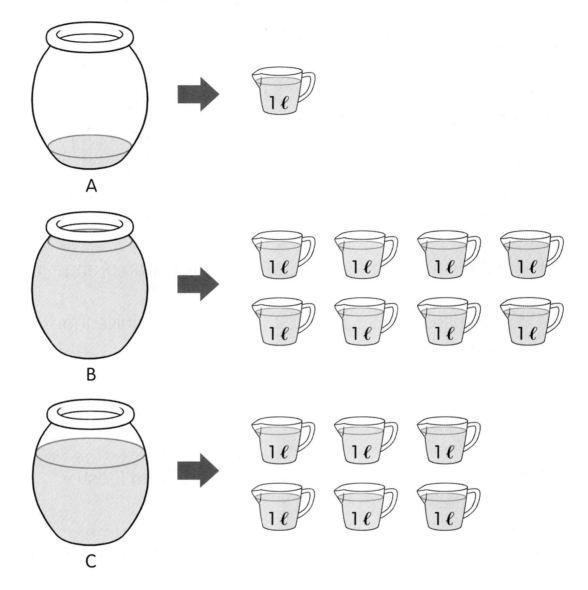

(a) Container B has _____ ℓ of water.

(b) Container C has _____ ℓ of water.

(c) Arrange the containers from the smallest to the greatest volume of water.

_____, _____, _____
smallest

Practice 3   Addition and Subtraction of Volumes

Solve.

(1)   Mrs Chen brought 96 ℓ of fruit juice to a birthday party.
After the birthday party, 16 ℓ of fruit juice was left.
How much fruit juice was drunk at the party?

_____ ℓ of fruit juice was drunk at the party.

(2)   Amir had two fish tanks.
He filled one tank with 15 ℓ of water and
the other tank with 9 ℓ of water.
How much water did he use to fill the two tanks altogether?

He used _____ ℓ of water to fill the two tanks altogether.

Lesson 3   Addition and Subtraction of Volumes

(3) Container A has 18 ℓ of water.
Container B has 5 ℓ of water more than Container A.
Container C has 16 ℓ of water less than Container B.

(a) How much water is there in Container B?
(b) How much water is there in Container C?

(a)

There are _____ ℓ of water in Container B.

(b)

There are _____ ℓ of water in Container C.

(4) Sophia has 23 ℓ of apple juice.
Sophia and Ryan have 57 ℓ of apple juice altogether.

(a) How many litres of apple juice does Ryan have?
(b) How many more litres of apple juice does Ryan have than Sophia?

(a)

Ryan has _____ ℓ of apple juice.

(b)

Ryan has _____ ℓ more apple juice than Sophia.

(5) Richard sold 54 ℓ of tea in a day.
Bella sold 29 ℓ of tea less than Richard.
How many litres of tea did they sell altogether?

They sold _____ ℓ of tea altogether.

Practice 4   Multiplication and Division of Volumes

Solve.

(1)   Mrs Heng's family drinks 6 ℓ of milk in a week.
How many litres of milk does her family drink in 3 weeks?

Her family drinks _____ ℓ of milk in 3 weeks.

(2)   Kamil pours 35 ℓ of syrup equally into 5 containers.
How much syrup is there in each container?

There are _____ ℓ of syrup in each container.

(3)   Kavita poured 36 ℓ of oil into some bottles.
Each bottle contained 4 ℓ of oil.
How many bottles did Kavita use altogether?

Kavita used _____ bottles altogether.

(4) Fatimah has 4 fish tanks.
She fills each fish tank with 3 ℓ of water.
How much water is there in all the fish tanks?

There are _____ ℓ of water in all the fish tanks.

(5) Mr Goh's pet cat drinks 2 ℓ of milk each week.
How many weeks does his cat take to drink 14 ℓ of milk?

His cat takes _____ weeks to drink 14 ℓ of milk.

(6) Banu filled a barrel with 16 ℓ of water.
Then, she poured the water into 4 pails equally.
How much water was there in each pail?

There were _____ ℓ of water in each pail.

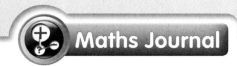

Maths Journal

Use the words to write an addition or subtraction story.

| Tank A | 45 ℓ | more |
| Tank B | 5 ℓ | |

_____

_____

_____

_____

_____

Show your working here.

Name: _____ Class: _____ Date: _____

 **Performance Task**

Your teacher gives out two containers labelled A and B.

(a) Fill each container with 1 ℓ of water using measuring cups.
Guess the amount of water each container can hold.

Container A can hold about _____ ℓ.

Container B can hold about _____ ℓ.

(b) Measure the amount of water each container can hold using measuring cups.
Record the actual amount of water in each container.

Container A has about _____ ℓ.

Container B has about _____ ℓ.

(c) Which container has more water?

Container _____ has more water.

Put on Your Thinking Cap!

  Challenging Practice

Fill in the blanks.

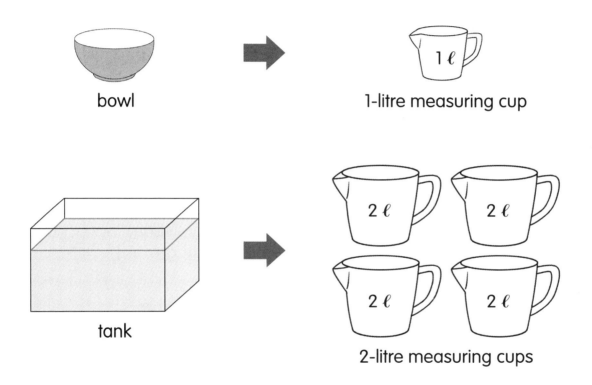

(a) How many bowls of water does it take to fill a 2-litre measuring cup?

_____

(b) How many bowls of water does it take to fill the tank?

_____

Name: _____ Class: _____ Date: _____

Problem Solving

Jasmine is a scientist.
She made a new liquid called Liquid X.
On the first day, she made 2 ℓ of Liquid X.
On the second day, she made 1 ℓ more of Liquid X than on the first day.
Every day, she made 1 ℓ more than the day before.

How much Liquid X did she make on Day 5?

Try **making a list** or **drawing a diagram**.

Name: _____ Class: _____ Date: _____

Revision 2

Section A

Read the questions.
Each question has four options.
Choose the correct option (❶, ❷, ❸ or ❹).
Write the number in the brackets provided.

(1)　5 hundreds and 6 ones written in numerals is _____.
　　　❶ 506　　　❷ 560
　　　❸ 605　　　❹ 650　　　　　　　　　　　　　　　　（　）

(2)　Which of the following is correct?
　　　❶ In 345, the digit 3 is in the ones place.
　　　❷ In 345, the digit 5 is in the ones place.
　　　❸ In 345, the digit 5 is in the tens place.
　　　❹ In 345, the digit 4 is in the hundreds place.　　（　）

(3)　_____ is 100 less than 815.
　　　❶ 715　　　❷ 805
　　　❸ 816　　　❹ 915　　　　　　　　　　　　　　　　（　）

(4)　Farmer Heng has 456 chickens.
　　　He has 120 fewer ducks than chickens.
　　　How many ducks does Farmer Heng have?
　　　❶ 120　　　❷ 336
　　　❸ 576　　　❹ 792　　　　　　　　　　　　　　　　（　）

Revision 2

(5)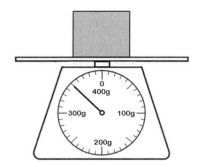

The mass of the box is _____.
① 370 g   ② 350 g
③ 330 g   ④ 300 g   (   )

(6) String A is 45 cm long.
String B is 71 cm long.
How much longer is String B than String A?
① 26 cm   ② 34 cm
③ 36 cm   ④ 116 cm   (   )

(7) Sumin bought a violin for $287.
She gave the cashier $500.
How much change did Sumin get?
① $213   ② $287
③ $313   ④ $387   (   )

(8)

Which is the correct amount of the money shown?
① $150.30   ② $150.60
③ $156.60   ④ $200.60   (   )

(9) Jiahui finished her dinner at 6.00 p.m.
She went for a walk after her dinner.
She came home 30 minutes later.
Which of the clocks below shows the time Jiahui reached home?

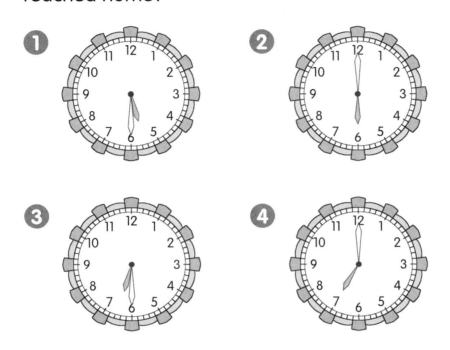

( )

(10) Fandi makes 24 ℓ of lemonade for his class party.
He makes 5 ℓ more of lemonade.
Jessie makes 12 ℓ of orange juice.
How much more lemonade than orange juice is there?
① 12 ℓ   ② 17 ℓ
③ 29 ℓ   ④ 41 ℓ

( )

(11) Which of the following shows fractions arranged from greatest to smallest?

① $\frac{1}{4}, \frac{4}{4}, \frac{3}{4}$ ② $\frac{4}{4}, \frac{1}{4}, \frac{2}{4}$

③ $\frac{1}{4}, \frac{2}{4}, \frac{4}{4}$ ④ $\frac{4}{4}, \frac{2}{4}, \frac{1}{4}$

( )

(12) A wire was made into a square as shown.
What was the total length of the wire used?

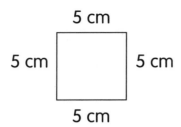

① 5 cm
② 10 cm
③ 15 cm
④ 20 cm   (   )

(13) Elsie's teacher told her to shade $\frac{7}{12}$ of the rectangle.
Look at Elsie's work.

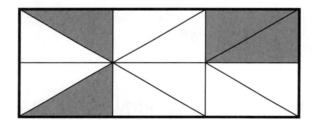

Her teacher told her to check her answer.
Why?

① She shaded $\frac{8}{12}$ of the rectangle.

② She shaded $\frac{3}{12}$ of the rectangle.

③ She shaded $\frac{4}{12}$ of the rectangle.

④ She has to add more triangles to make
$\frac{7}{12}$ of the rectangle.   (   )

Section B

Read the questions carefully.
Work out the answers and write them in the blanks provided.

(14) What fraction of the figure is shaded?

Answer: _____

(15) What comes next?
Circle the correct shape.

 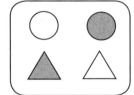

(16) The wallet shows how much money John has.
He spends $3.
How much money is left in his wallet now?

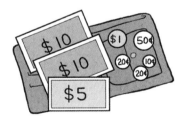

Answer: $_____

(17) What is the missing number?

$21 \div $ 🌸 $= 3$

🌸 = _____

Answer: _____

(18) How much longer is String B than String A?

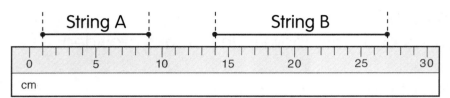

Answer: _____ cm

(19) What is the missing sign in the box?

36 ☐ 4 = 9

Answer: _____

(20) What is the missing number?

```
   2  6  ☐
-  1  8  4
_____
         7  7
```

Answer: _____

(21) Draw a line 11 cm long.

(22) Vera bought two bottles of soya bean milk.
Each bottle contained 2 ℓ of soya bean milk.
How much soya bean milk did Vera buy altogether?

Answer: _____ ℓ

(23) A jug contained 6 ℓ of syrup.
2 ℓ of syrup was poured out.
How much syrup was left in the jug?

Answer: _____ ℓ

(24) Four people are in a queue to buy food.
Alex is in front of Farhan.
Tricia is behind Hazel and in front of Alex.
Who is second in the queue?

Answer: _____

(25) Mei Fong started cooking dinner at 4.30 p.m.
She spent 1 hour cooking.
Draw the hands to show the time she ended her cooking.

Use the picture graph to answer questions 26 to 27.

At a school funfair, Min set up a stall to sell cupcakes.
The picture graph shows the number of each type of cupcake sold.
Study the picture graph.
Then, fill in the blanks.

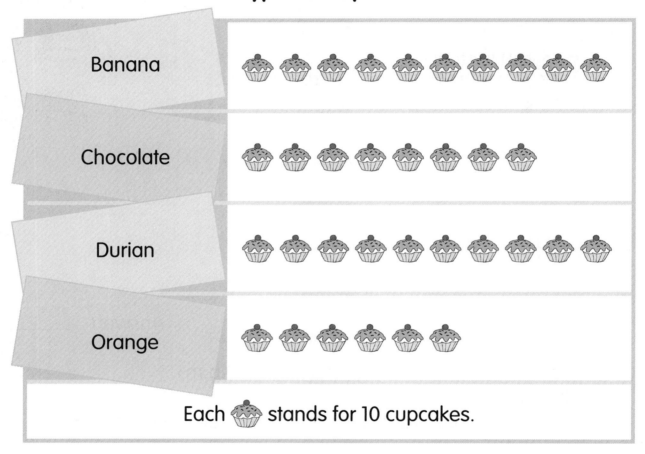

(26) She sold _____ orange cupcakes.

(27) She sold _____ more durian cupcakes than chocolate cupcakes.

Section C

Read the questions carefully.
Show all your workings in the spaces provided.

(28) Lily bought 6 pails.
Each pail could hold 4 ℓ of water.
Lily filled all the pails completely with water.
How many litres of water were there in all the pails?

(29) Mr Aziz had 84 kg of flour.
He sold 31 kg of flour.
How much flour had he left?

(30) Pauline has $210.
James has $36 more than Pauline.
James gives Pauline $50.
How much does James have now?

(31) Rope A is 17 cm long.
The total length of Ropes A and B is 32 cm.
The total length of Ropes B and C is 33 cm.
What is the length of Rope C?

BLANK